THIRST

Thirst

Michael Glover

Copyright © Michael Glover 2025
The moral rights of the author have been asserted.

Acknowledgements
Achill Soundings was first published as a limited-edition book
by Red Fox Press, Achill Island; the *Tablet*
Drawings and monoprints accompanying 'Achill Soundings'
reproduced by courtesy Ruth Dupré
Artworks accompanying 'Webern' are by Michael Glover
Painting facing 'Thirst'
reproduced by courtesy of Joseph Glover
Cover painting, 'A Flourish of Pineapples'
reproduced by courtesy of Ruth Dupré

www.1889books.co.uk
ISBN: 978-1-915045-50-8

Other publications by Michael Glover

Poetry :

Measured Lives (1994)
Impossible Horizons (1995)
A Small Modicum of Folly (1997)
The Bead-Eyed Man (1999)
Amidst All This Debris (2001)
For the Sheer Hell of Living (2008)
Only So Much (2011)
Hypothetical May Morning (2018)
Messages to Federico (2018)
What You Do With Days (2019)
One Season in Hell (2020)
The Timely Lift-Off of the Famous Harlequin-Fish (2022)
What Turns Up (2022)
The Skittery Zipper (2023)
Mistaking You for a Shower of Summer Confetti (2024)
Where We Left Off (with Jason Heroux) (2024)
Vincent's Poets (2024)

Others :

Headlong into Pennilessness (2011)
Great Works: Encounters with Art (2016)
Playing Out in the Wireless Days (2017)
111 Places in Sheffield You Shouldn't Miss (2017)
Late Days (2018)
Neo Rauch (2019)
The Book of Extremities (2019)
Thrust (2019)
John Ruskin: an idiosyncratic dictionary (2019)
Rose Wylie (2020)
Whose? (2020)
The Trapper (2021)
Nellie's Devils and Other Stories (2022)

794 Mini Sagas (2023)
111 Hidden Art Treasures of London (2024)
Cambridge Central Mosque (2024)
Searching for Ezra (2025)

As editor or contributor :

Memories of Duveen Brothers (1976)
Goin' down, down, down: Matthew Ronay (2006)
Between Eagles and Pioneers: Georg Baselitz (2011)
Robert Therrien (2016)
Monique Frydman (2017)
A Garland of Poems for Christmas (with Martyn Crucefix) (2022)
Van Gogh: Poets and Lovers (2024)

Contents

Good afternoon Ada	1
Achill Soundings	4
Webern: a poem-cycle	36
A Steady Downpour	102
Violets	114
Reeds in the Wind	134
One Daughter to Another: A Garland of Fourteen Poems in Loving Memory	150
Dear Bill *(i.m. William Carlos Williams)*	166
Escapology	190
Thirst	200

For Ada, and her bounty of promises…

Good Afternoon, Ada

Tiny head cupped
near weightless,
in the palm

(my palm
almost enfolding it)…

Her lips part
(flower buds opening
at spring's beckoning),

but not to speak.
It is a soundless parting…

How delicate pink
her eyelids are!
(those too unstirring)

Then, a drama, sudden –
Her mouth skews,
tiny head judders.

And the cry, when it comes,
is barely a cry at all,
more a thin, high piping

From some distant valley's bottom

Achill Soundings

The Presence of Kelp

A wash of haphazard air
stirs the kelp on the kitchen table.
It has been drying for a day now.
When you lifted it with such care
from Golden Strand Beach,
It hung across your forearm
like a wet sleeve of heavy fabric.

Now, drier, this airy, translucent form
is lighter altogether,
as, little by little,
it crisps and releases its full range of colours –
a veiny indigo green, for example,
but most of all an entire spectrum
Of chocolatey browns.

Its long tapering form
thins at both ends.
One disappears in a mild,
ever more thinning fritter.
The other concludes
in a playful, bob-shaped tassel.
Were you a jester,
I might invite you to make it jingle.

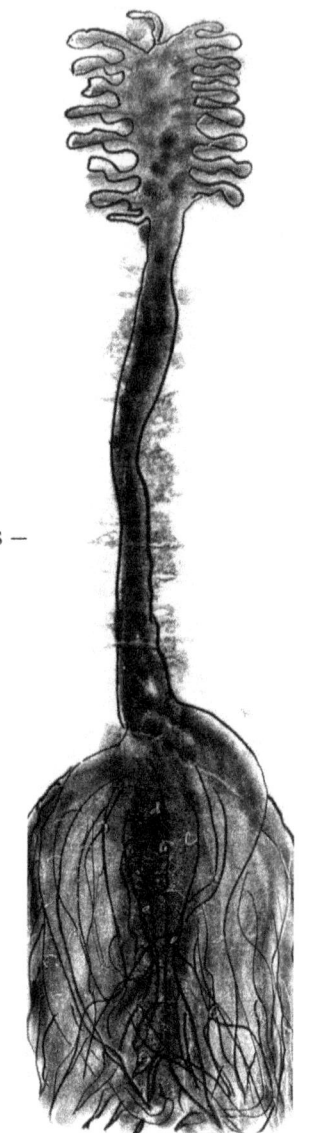

Letter to Heinrich Böll

Heinrich (if I may so familiarly address you),
the unexpected gift of a residency
finds me today in the kitchen
of your beautiful Irish cottage
in Dugort, Achill Island,
off a steep and narrow lane
overlooking Blacksod Bay.

Thank you for the pleasure of your company,
I whisper to your ghost
as I settle into the chair
behind the long, smooth reach
of your writing table.
Reared up to the left of me, an old, glazed bookcase
opens to reveal your Collected Works in German,
all twenty-six volumes of them
in their discreet red bindings.

Once I have cleared at a single leap
the high, barred gate that separates me
from the most rudimentary knowledge of German,
I shall doubtless set about reading them.
In the interim, I satisfy my more limited ambitions
by leafing through various volumes of your fiction
in English translation (there are several of them here),
and a book about your perilous voyage to Ireland
in 1955, your residency, and your subsequent reflections upon
The Irish Question – if an Englishman, stepping delicately,
may so call it...

So you are here with me today
as I open my loose-leaf notebook,
and stare, helplessly, at the yawning promise
of the very first of many blank pages to be filled.
Ranged in front of me are the few books – Nietzsche, Villon,
Pound, Bonnefoy, Herodotus and Burton's *Anatomy of Melancholy* –
which I decided to carry along with me from London

as thinking companions, the kinds of works
I regarded as appropriate
to this high-minded literary occasion.
In which direction to travel though?
That is the most pressing question.

I receive no good advice whatsoever
from the temperament of these sheep,
who are clearly the ragged kings and queens of this island.
The way they weave about the road
as cars purr in a single long line behind them
reveals that their business is to please none but themselves.
I cannot pose or posture as a sheep
in the short time allotted to me here.
I must settle on a trajectory of my own,
beat out phrases of moment on the brain's anvil
with fury and decisiveness.

Heinrich, I do not expect you to help me.
In fact, might not your overwhelming
presence here even be a bit of a hinderance?
You have done your work, and it is a mighty monument.
My pen trembles as it hovers over this empty page.
Have you not already outdistanced me?

Hold steady though. The rain is slowing.
Even on Achill, on such a day as this one,
there is the delicious promise of evening sunshine

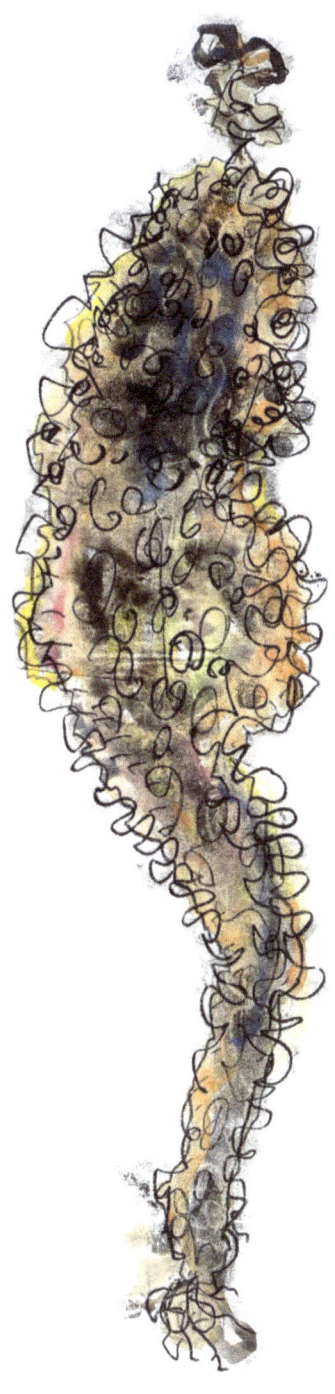

Swimming from Gielty's Bar

I left home from this spot here,
right beside Gielty's Bar,
breasting the Atlantic
on the year's most lashing day,
every inch the true Achill man.

You thought I would need a boat.
Ha! I gave up on those long ago.
Remember how I stamped the sand as a babe,
when you all pointed, and said –
there's the legs of a true, coming Achill man!

Where you headed then, boy?
they all asked, not a little curious,
as I stood, flexing and staring out.
Where else but Newfoundland? I said,
to find the old ones,

those of former days,
who never made it back
to tell us what went on.
Is not that the task
of any true Achill man?

Remember those wakes, so sad,
when they waved them off,
as tears were shed?
I'm bringing them all back,
to tell it as it was,
as any true Achill man would.

And then they let me go.

A Complaint Addressed to Mount Slievemore

Slievemore, you have never been
a natural conversationalist.
Why must you hide your head
in a fug of mist
when I address you,
inviting you to speak out
on the prospects for this,
your island home?

Why did you cause me to twist
and then turn my ankle
on your lower slopes?
Why choose to pivot North
when I was headed West?
Was it malice, indifference or worse?
If you would only suffer me to buy
your Collected Works in Irish,
I might then begin to comprehend you.

Roadside Sheep

Not all sheep are dandies, well turned out
into a road from a field uneven and tussocky,
brandishing thistles. More often they sit down together
in twos or threes, or tuck themselves into a handy slope
beside the tarmac, where the traffic goes so reverentially slow.
Are these Achill sheep or New Delhi cows?
You may well wonder.

Most of all, they mind their own business,
and potter off whenever it suits them,
on the latest flighty notion, to go.
They sit, stand, or challenge if we get too close,
with that deadpan stare from their burning yellow eyes.
All leads precisely nowhere of course,
because we all veer away out of sheer politeness,

yet waiting, always, to spot them again,
some wide and swaying as well fleeced barrels,
others, almost cabaret, finicky and skinny-legged
in tight black raiment, who will settle for a while
nowhere in particular, tired perhaps
to have a lamb forever in tow,
butting and flustering, god damn it, to feed –
the no holds barred comedy of bouncy, blustery slobber

Drowning in Lough Acorrymore

An almighty glacial shift
once scooped out this bowl of a lake
in the mountains. This is
where my father used to escape to,
seeking the freedom to hunt for wild goats –
and just register the angle of the incline!
How he would climb and climb
to escape the grinding civil service routine
that was, life-long, his weekday job's burden…
Needless to say, he never found one.

I have brought you up here
to show this off to you, amongst the very best
that there is of Achill Island,
one of the sacred places of my early childhood.
We enjoyed such free-roaming days back then.
Hadn't a clue where we were, the parents.
All they said was: be back before the rosary, children.
And so we were, bruised, battered, and always happy,
never a care in God's world
or a thought in the head either.
I call it to this day a perfect childhood

I quite forgot to mention:
on that bank over there, that's where
that poor, stuttery child of a boy-man –
he got an Oscar for best supporting actor –
proposed to her in the film, do you remember?
Needless to say, she said no.
The next thing we know, they are lifting
his body from the water.
You watch it again when you have a moment.
It is almost heart-stopping…
Shall we descend now for lunch?
I'm sure you're as peckish as I am.

An Irish Emigrant in the 1950s

I still try to come to terms
with the sadness of it all
on those dark, dawn winter mornings,
hearing the slow to-and-fro foot shuffle
of those women in the lane below,
quietly sobbing behind the hedgerow,
as I lay in my bed, too far away to see,
and too close not to always hear it all.

It always began the previous evening,
with the steady clop, clop of the donkey
pulling its load up the lane,
and settling with a long snort beside our back gate.
Then off it would be dropped from the cart,
a solid trunk full of any boy's lifetime's belongings.
We barely looked. We never stepped out.
We certainly never touched it.
It would have felt superstitious to do so.

The dawn made sense of it all.
First the low talk from two or three or more,
followed, soon enough, by the bus
into which trunk, and then boy
would, with a quick leap, disappear.
We would hear it pulling away,
gears clattering, before that long hard uphill heave.
And then it would begin, the wailing and the sobbing,
for just as long as forever always takes.

White Bechstein in Sea Mist

The mist rolls in relentlessly across this island.
Some scarcely notice.
Two young Americans,
idealists both of them,
spell-bound by this place and its music,
once made a home for themselves in
a mountain-top fastness,
with piano by way of companion.

Pure folly, as it happens.
Did no local once think to whisper:
mist makes for tunelessness?
The piano tuner visited every day thereafter.
Up and down he went,
from valley to mountain
and then back again.

The ignorance of the American
remains unfathomable.

Climbing Slievemore's Southern Flank
Towards the Deserted Village

A bleakly exposed mountain slope
as steeply uprearing as this one
makes for a slow, twisty, stumbling climb for all
but these enviably nimble-footed sheep
who agilely leap from stone to uneven stone
on their approach to this long abandoned village.
The wind's push-back is both defiant and tremendous.

Only some ruinous walls remain these days
of these tiny, embattled houses
in front of which today young girls pose,
laughing and joshing, before running on.
The fuller human story is long gone.

Could any of those who lived here once,
before famine drove so many down valley
and into the perilously welcoming arms
of Keel's great, out-flung bay,
be settled by chance in
Dugort's old walled cemetery next door?

No. The dead mourned there are too newly passed
to be contenders, and far too well-to-do.
No smoking peat fires for honoured dead such as these,
who can afford the protective pomp
of a black marble table-top tomb,
with its hearts, good wishes, and the bust
of a leaning angel paying homage.

Sheep in Mist

Creeping along the slow coastal road
from Keel to Dooagh this late Friday afternoon,
dreaming of eating wild Atlantic clam chowder
(Starter deftly upgraded to Main)
from a table carefully positioned
at the handy look-out of a window seat
in Gielty's Bar ('the most westerly eating place
on the whole of Achill Island')
which faces the rain-slicked car park,
where the green (needless to say)
Banshees of Innisherin tour coach habitually parks,
tucked tight into the hedge
thanks to the local driver's wealth of local knowledge,

I notice, steadily going like the most patient
of weather-attuned, sheep-aware drivers,
that the ceiling of the sky has dramatically lowered
since this morning, and that it is surely
all this ever relentlessly onward-rolling sea mist
which has done it, changed, at a stroke,
our entire perspective upon this our breathing world,
robbed us of shoreline, mountains,
the heady prospect of any distant horizon.

Are not all our expectations thereby reduced,
as if suffering some curse?
Are we not ducked down and shrunken,,
fearing the worst that might yet be to come,
reduced to this common level of quivery timorousness,
now that the whole of the sky and even much of this
seeable island has been withdrawn from us?
Are we not less than we once were,
wholly diminished men, women, boys and girls,
mere tatterdemalion remnants of our former selves?

And does this stray sheep, here by the road just spotted,
know of any of this? In fact, is not its steady cud-chewing
much as it always was? Has it then always known much more
than we sad mortals would ever presume to encompass?
Why then, in that case though, would God,
in the presumption of his mercy, so abase us all?

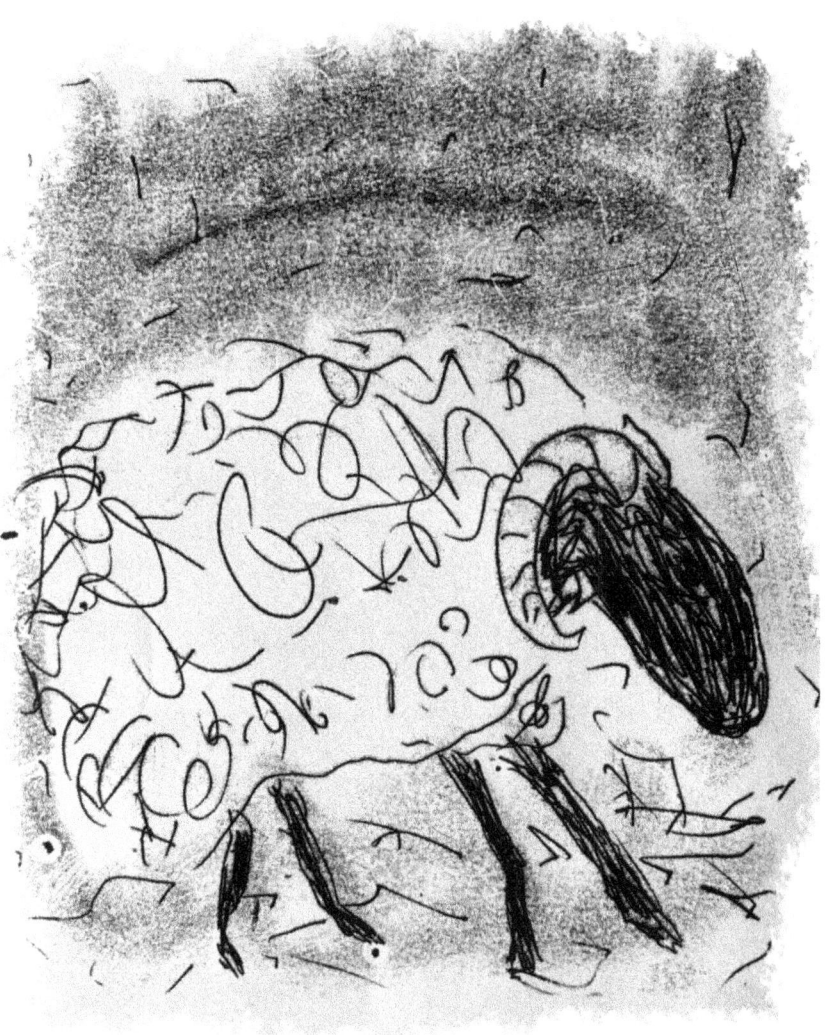

Pure Black Magic

The photographer has caught the boy to perfection
at the moment when the wave lifts his surf board
into a buckingly steep upward incline,
              almost clear of the ever onrushing
turbulence of the waters, so that his head rises too,
and his hair, at a near perfectly sculpted angle…

Where I am seated to be witnessing such marvels?
At a table, in the ocean-facing front parlour of Pure Magic,
the pizza restaurant within sight of Keel Bay,
where that magical balancing act
would almost certainly have taken place,

sculpting a pizza into near perfect triangles,
one of the best I have ever eaten,
fashioned from onion, bacon, and melted mozzarella,
with a fried egg on the pivot at its centre,
the turning sun of its yoke staring up at me,
at which I smile down in happy acknowledgement
of the sheer succulence of its virtues.

My only trouble is its name, which I repeat
back at you now so that I can share
my mixture of unease and perplexity.
Why call this puffy-cheeked, golden-brown
perfectly circular creation Mount Slievemore Pizza
in the first place? I grant you there could be
justification of sorts based on raw proximity.

Slievemore's indomitable flank looms over the back
of this place – I can almost feel
the heft of her pressing against my shoulders.
And will she not always rise up in such a way,
the threat, and the warn, and even the threatening
gloom of her habitually mist-shrouded presence?

What though has she to do with the nature, the fashioning,
or even the finished form of a smoothly edible
pizza of the kind I am just now eating?
Has some witless, puff-ball-brained chef
thrown down, thanks to this reckless act of idle name-calling,
what could in fact amount to a taunt
which will, in the fullness of time, be profoundly regretted?

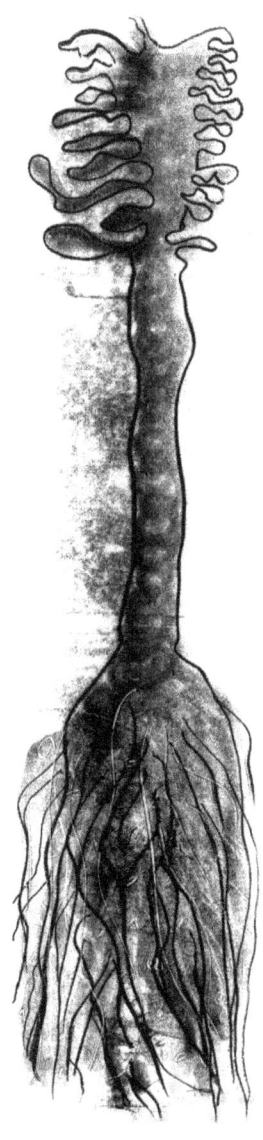

Remembrance in Dugort

Heinrich, I am this morning contentedly settled
in front of your window, tap-tapping
on the long leather reach of your desk
which gives onto, this bright Monday morning,

such natural marvels – not though the fuschia hedge
which once blocked the view from here
down to the curve of the bay and the ever more
generous spread of its feisty waters.

It was here, to Dugort, that the Protestants came
back in the 1840s, to do some good,
and to spread the word of their plain-speaking god.
Needless to say, their presence here was not universally welcomed.

Food came, together with words of unwelcome exhortation
to eschew the Babylonian woe – as furious Milton once put it.
The bishop spat back, creating a monastery at Bunacurry,
Mission Schools, together with some violence
            and much indignation.

Now, here at Dugort, at the end of a long
            and darkly embowered lane,
the little Protestant church still stands, locked away and silent.
Some of that persuasion still live and quietly die here though –
the hump of a fresh turned grave in the graveyard

behind the back of the high altar spills today with a cascade
of new laid flowers, around which
all may gather and take pleasure
in remembrance of the life of Alison Jane McMullen.

Breakfast at The Bervie
for John and Liz

Outside, on this most dramatic morning of mornings,
rain pummels mercilessly at the windows
like the spectre of some leering, raving ghoulie.
Indoors, in the dining room of The Bervie,
it is the case of a quiet succession of ceremonious offerings,
beginning with the table-settings:

here for your delectation is willow-pattern
in its full-blown dream of
extravagant Regency Anglo-Chinoiserie –
from rising pagoda to dream-struck bridge-crossers
and casually winging swallows – for tea cups and plates;
silver service for hot milk and coffee;

cruets for salt and pepper as amorously close
as two love-birds in an over-tight embrace;
snub-nosed butter knife balanced across butter pats
the size and the shape of sheep droppings
out there in the lane;

and all backed by stippled wallpaper
of an almost lickable lemony yellow;
with the window drapes at our back held in place
by ropes knotted into a symmetrical pairing of loose, fat bows,
giving on to a table set for six out on a verandah
presided over by a jug of nicely appointed hydrangeas…

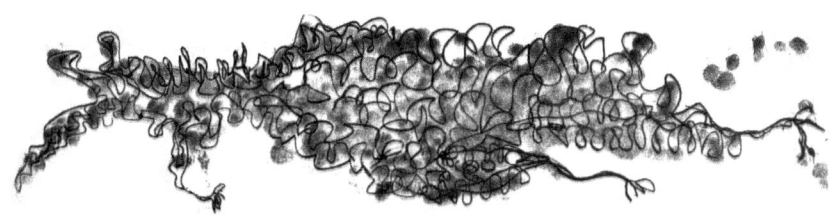

And the rain goes on lashing and lashing,
as it surely must and ever will,
demanding a glum, if not angry, defiance from
those it counts as its victims.
It does not get its way.
In the dining room of the Bervie,
no one, but no one, succumbs.
There is too much pleasure
on this morning of mornings
in all the giving and the taking.

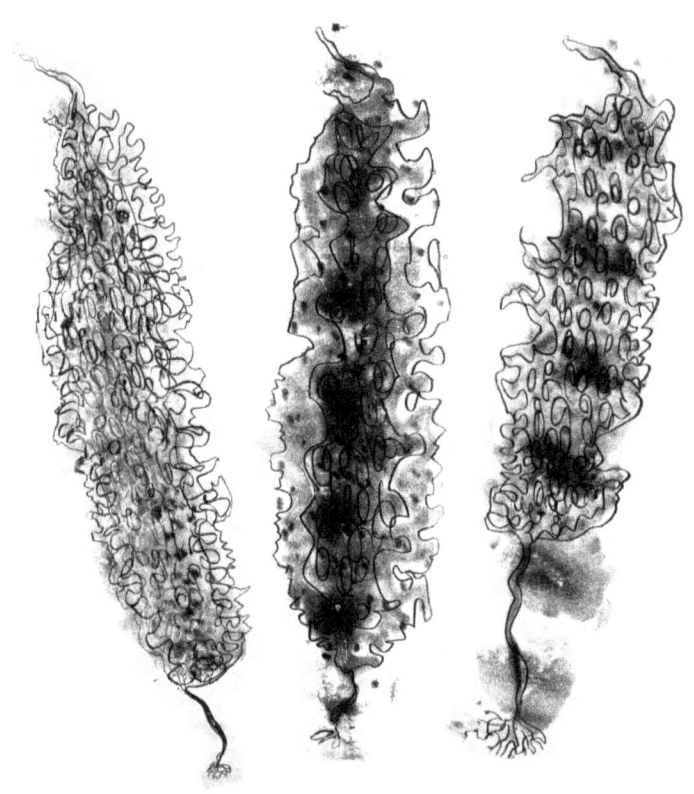

The Meaning of the Stones of Dookinella

It often all seems to go, vanishes quite away,
in an outbreath of air,
what exactly you may think you are seeking
when you exclaim out into the air,
to another who just happens to be there,
ears cocked, listening,
that you have arrived just there
at the junction where a pub sign has told you:
open Thursday to Sunday, with music
if you are lucky. And are you not always lucky
at a junction such as this one,
with the sunshine making its brightness felt
on your hair, having dispelled all the clouds
of early morning? Are you not now,
as you thought, here in Dookinella,
where you had expected to be arriving?

And so you go on for a while,
driving and driving, weaving and twisting
between a modest strew of sun-struck holiday homes,
because a lane such as this one
is never a straight one,
just as thinking is never straight either,
the nature of thinking that is,
but what is it exactly that you are thinking
this morning? And where exactly had you expected
to be arriving, after all this tedious
driving and driving,
which had felt, from moment to moment,
so random, but most certainly wasn't

because Dookinella was always the destination.
And here now is Dookinella itself,
and it is a quiet, mid-day moment
which you are at last inhabiting,
where children in that schoolyard
you have just passed by

on that hill slope up to the left
have been passing a ball from one to another
by way of a little light relief
from the tedium of their lessons.

And you no more look up at them
as you drive past than they look down at you
because each one of us is bounded by his own preoccupations.
And so it is here at last, Dookinella,
and the long bay, with its islands beyond,
is stretched out in front of you,
and this haze of an ocean,
now glittering, now sullen,
with, to the left, these cliffs fine and upstanding,
by way of an offering, a promise.

What exactly is here for you though?
What meaning can be invested in a word
so mellifluously lulling as Dookinella?
It is a matter of stones,
a spasmodic patterning of stones,
and how they are configured
on a rising hillside, this is where you are headed,
stones in a pattern
not even to be seen
until, almost by chance, you come upon them,
having first followed the haphazard way of all
these island sheep who never seem quite to know
where they are going until they pause and feed
in a newly seized mood of contentment.

You do not, you cannot, share such a mood of contentment
because you have thought beyond their thinking
precisely in order to be here this morning,
you have wanted to see for yourself
what meaning this pattern holds for you,
this loose, spasmodic patterning of bright white quartz fragments,
so many dots in the form of an almost square,
with a stone cross at its centre,
and, at top left, a small cairn topped by an angel.

Here is where they took them, babe upon babe,
unwanted chattels, unbaptised, cast out,
never part of the story.
They brought them here, all the mothers,
under cover of darkness, and buried them
to form a tiny gathering of the lost and the unwanted
up on this hillside,
and, much later, the ocean rose up and seized them,
I fancifully imagine,
and swept off their bones,
to be discovered, bleached and water-baptised, later
much, much later.
And that is the meaning of Dookinella.

That, in short or long, is the meaning of your Dookinella.
Squeeze it now to yourself, ever closer and closer.

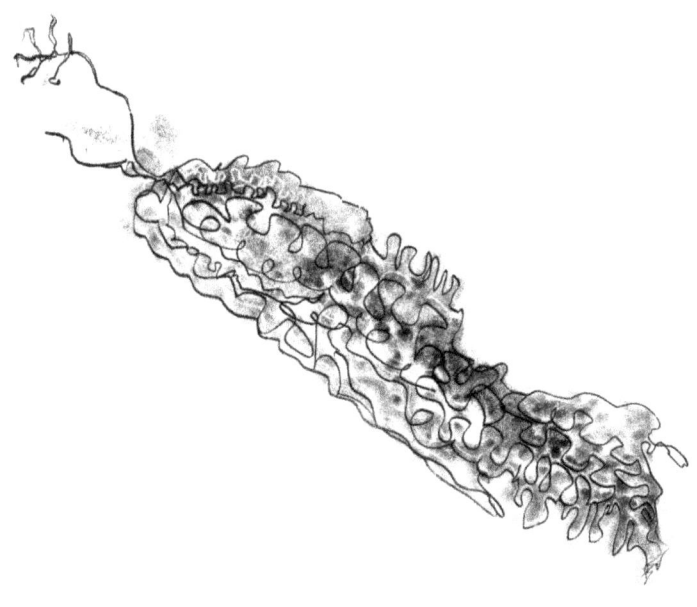

Looking out from Heinrich's Writing Room

The field in front of my eyes
is so ragged, jostly and boisterously unkempt
when the wind combs through it,
with its range of thistles, grasses, rushes,
hunkered down shrubs and bushes,
and its lovely declivities – its humps and its falls,
its twists and its swerves –
so unexpected, that it proves

quite difficult to raise one's gaze
to the ocean's broad and level plain
scarcely half a mile away
down the lane in Blacksod Bay,
with the hills of Ballycroy beyond,
so reticently pale this morning,
and so vaguely soothing to the gaze.

And yet the writing must go on, and so it is
with some reluctance that I draw my look back
to this desk at the window
and my narrow stockade of books,
all but one of them written in English
(or translated into the same),
lest the noise of Heinrich's
germanic symphonies in prose
in this bookcase beside me
drown out all thinking,
and cause me to run wild, arms flapping,
out into the garden,
as if my brain had just now combusted.

Returning Seaweed to the Ocean

Dead, alive, or some in-between state?
Weed, animal or what?
Fantastical rope of sorts?
Or some wild and unruly improvisation
upon the nature of pasta?
How to describe such a wet and ungovernable,
slithery stretch of frilly bunchings
and fat, wet striplets of green matter?

Not to be denied was the fact
of her being, to my mind, so stinkingly repulsive.
which is why I took no pleasure
in the way you gathered her all up from the beach
behind the Bervie, and bundled her into a plastic bag
without hesitation or ceremony.

And then so carefully laid her out like a sprawled drunk
across the bench in the courtyard
as if something would come of her one day.
What though? Was she even drawable?
And would not the stench, the sour sea-reek of her,
forever remain with us?

And so it is that this morning
I watch with calmness and pleasure
the sight of you picking your way
down the rocks to ocean's edge
at Doeega, that old fishing village
on the wild western coast of the island.
and I watch you as you turn her out on to the sand
and arrange her for the future with a tenderness
which is truly beyond
both my reach and my comprehension.

Contemplating the presence of Grainne at Greenwich Palace from a lane overlooking Achill Sound

Let us stand then, having leant
our bikes against this wall,
and take stock for a moment.
Nothing happens just here
on the stillness of a summer's morning.
nothing has ever happened.
You just pause here and stare

at the old squat tower of Kildownet Castle
facing out to the Sound
from where Grainne, an Irish warrior queen
once played the dangerous game of piracy,
cat-and-mousing with English foes
to such a needling extent
that the Virgin Queen herself
granted her an audience
to petition for the lives of her captive sons.

Yes, she would meet her
on condition that the two queens
must always be on an equal footing.
And so it proved to be, at Greenwich Palace…
at which point, having wiped the sweat from our foreheads,
we take up our bicycles and face forward and into
the upcoming challenge of the mountains.

Returning to the scene of the filming of the Banshees of Inisherin by the coastal road from Keel

I was a driver you see, John says,
turning back to face me from the driving seat.
Then he flicks a quick finger spray of holy water
directly into my shocked face
from what I take to be a whisky flask or some such,
for good luck's sake.

        Off we are going to Keem Bay
to see where it was shot, and – mother of all mercies! –
how that coastal drive, from Keel and on West,
brings it all back!

        That, he says,
as we reach a curve in the road
overlooking the beach where so much of it was shot,
is where they had the mobile restaurant.
There was so much food, for everyone, and all day too –
such apples, pears, bananas and oranges
to stretch an entire lifetime of credibility!

Parked now above the little house itself,
above the beach where the old man brooded
beside the fire, nurturing their feud,
we set off down that unnervingly steep
and boggy hillside at quite a young goat's gallop.

        The house itself is boarded up,
and the pub, of course, where the argufying
and the drinking and the fiddling took place,
never ever was – it was made for the occasion only,
plopped down on the other side of the island,
and taken off to Galway, all gone
as if nothing had ever happened,
two weeks after the filming had ended.
Such is the nature of things, John tells us

with a long shake of the head before he snatches the phone
from our hands to snap us at the back of the cottage
for the sake of the oceanward direction.
He kneels as if in church on suckably damp earth
for the sake of the perfect shot.

No, the actors were not friendly,
except for the bit-part ones who were in his bus.
They were affable enough. Not the main ones though,
who always kept themselves to themselves,
of which John does not at all approve, he tells us.
It is always nice to be nice, he says,
as he asks me to get him in shot, smiling,
next to my wife, who is of course very obliging.

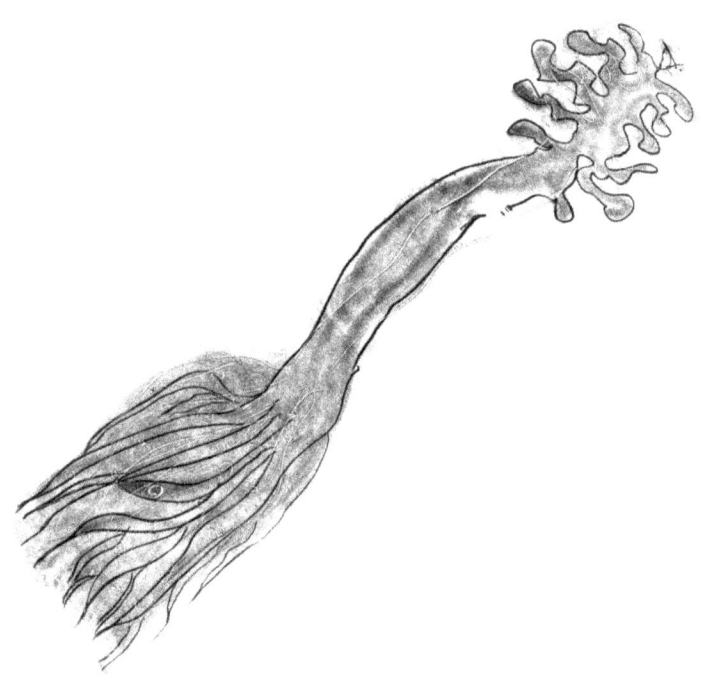

Afterword

The poems you have just read were written during a two-week writer's residency at the Heinrich Böll cottage on Achill Island in June of 2023.

Nothing turned out as expected. I had planned to devote my energies to a sequence of poems loosely based on those of François Villon. Ezra Pound had brought him afresh to my notice in May of that year when, in a garden in Andalucia, beneath the shade of a peppercorn tree more accustomed to giving safe harbour to chameleons, I had read the anthology Ezra edited late in life, in collaboration with perhaps the very last in a long string of young female admirers called Marcella Spann.

That anthology, published in 1964, was called *From Confucius to Cummings*, and it included versions of some poems by Villon written by the Victorian poet Algernon Charles Swinburne. Until I read those translations, I had never encountered a poem by Swinburne I thought deserved to be admired.

His versions of Villon were shockingly raw, painful and intimate. That discovery, together with a short piece by Pound on Villon in a book called *The Spirit of Romance*, quickened something in me, and persuaded me that my next creative endeavour should be to make my own versions of poems by Villon.

It was this project in the making that I carried over with me to Achill.

Once there, seated at Heinrich Böll's wonderful writing desk, I soon began to experience acute frustration for two quite separate reasons. The presence of Böll himself was far too present in that room – were not the twenty-six volumes of his collected works in German just to the left of me, in a fine glazed bookcase? And then there was the presence of Villon himself, his outrageous puns, his recondite vocabulary. What was to be done?

I retired to bed that evening at 8pm, exhausted and utterly dispirited. Of the presence of the island itself, I felt precisely nothing. It was merely a context.

Then, the following morning, something changed. Ruth and I went for a walk along Golden Strand beach, and it was there that she happened upon a piece of kelp the likes of which I had never before seen.

It looked like a rain-drenched, elegant foulard. We carried it back to the kitchen of the cottage. By the following morning it had dried into something crisp of texture and wondrously colourful – its range of browns, together with how those browns seemed to be shot through with dense indigo blues, stunned me.

There, on the kitchen table, without premeditation, I addressed a poem to that kelp.

That act of writing dispelled much of the tension I was feeling within myself, and seemed to release me to write, over the ensuing days of the residency, what I was seeing and feeling on Achill Island. I kept away from Heinrich's study for that first few days, working only at the kitchen table.

Half way through the residency, I felt sufficiently at ease with myself and my surroundings to return there, and write words I hoped would prove adequate to the occasion.

I conclude with the one response I made to the poetry of François Villon.

Michael Glover 30 June 2023

The Fair Armouress Regrets
(at some distance from the French of François Villon)

Tits shrivelled, thighs wasted,
disgustingly sold and re-sold,
I think back now to all those uproarious nights
trapped between stinking sheets,
when I was young and so quiveringly lean.

Who held me then?
At what price was such lust exacted?
Oh, am I not still that fair armouress of old
of which the great Francis Villon once wrote?
Can his degradation be the equal of my own?

I think back also to that song
to which he reduced me,
and of how he traduced me
in words as painful as they were slashingly bold.
He spared nothing of me.
He threw me at you
as one flings a bone towards which
every mutt in the neighbourhood bolts.

I am the fair armouress of old,
renowned for the bewitchment of my glances,
the seductiveness of my svelte low tones,
the sinuous lines of my body.
Admire me still, beneath these clothes,
in all the fine detailing towards which
your fingers might be inclined to wander
up hill and down those valleys of old.

Oh would it were then and not now!

Webern:
a poem-cycle

The Short Story of Anton Webern: a Foreword

A passion is a curious thing, often barely explicable or even understandable. I had discovered a passion for the music of the strangely austere, no-sooner-here-than-gone music of the Austrian composer Anton Webern (1883-1945) by the time that I was nineteen years old. I know that for a fact because it was in the autumn of 1968 that I took myself off to a hushed, culturally high-toned and rarified emporium called the Cambridge Music Shop on Trinity Street, and bought a boxed set of four long-playing records of his collected music as conducted by Robert Craft, who had been born in Kingston, New York State (a town I was later to get to know pretty well, though I never met Craft). This boxed set cost me a small fortune, and I regarded it as a jewel.

I would listen over and over to Webern's minutely-scaled pieces, and wonder about the fact that they seemed to exist in defiance of so much that I had come to expect of what is generally called classical music. There was no lushness, no grandiosity, no lulling sweep of strings, little intermeshing or interweaving of instrumental sound, and in fact very few customary flourishes of any kind whatsoever. His works were all so brief, so anguished, so fragmentary, so sharp, so astringent, so a-teeter on the edge of things. Was it even permissible for a self-sufficient piece of classical music to last no more than forty seconds? Well, why not though? And was it not on the edge of things that we nineteen-year-olds were all aspiring to live anyway?

I also committed an act of violation which still does not quite please me. That boxed set included a handsome booklet, with much musical analysis by Craft, the texts of the Lieder in English and German (half of Webern's output was written for the human voice), an aerial photograph of the village of Mittersill in an Alpine valley, where he is buried, and two portraits of him by Oscar Kokoschka, one a painting, the other a drawing. I cut out the drawing and pinned it to the wall of my room in Maid's Causeway so that Webern could watch over me. I later lost it, and so all that remains to me now is a booklet with a quarter page missing. And the cutting out was so lamentably crude! Only the caption has survived. The paintings in this book are my crude attempts to make reparations.

Webern's story was both small in dimensions and tragic. He had been a pupil of Arnold Schoenberg's in Vienna, a man he revered life-long, and he had then gone on to earn a small living of sorts as a tutor and a conductor. His later years were miserable and hounded. In the 1930s, the Nazis denounced this shy, modest man as a Bolshevik, a charge that could scarcely have been more ridiculous, and his early death at the end of the Second World War – an American soldier shot him (three bullets entered his body) for violating a curfew outside the house of his son-in-law in Mittersill – still feels like a kind of tragic mistake or a preposterous blunder. It was night time. He had been quietly smoking a cigar outside his door, at a forbidden hour. Webern may not even have known that a curfew had been imposed. Perhaps the trigger-happy soldier felt menaced by the sight of a glowing cigar tip in the dark.

And now all that we have left are the strange and often eerie consolations of his music. His entire oeuvre can be listened to in less than seven hours. These spiky poems try to bounce off that music, piece by piece, and represent a kind of wayward, blue-skies' tribute to the man and all that he has meant to me…

Passacaglia Op.1

In the interval, past waking,
and then to see again,
where all the waves folded in,
all at once,
and never for the asking.

Or to be spoken of too quickly,
past it all now,
just beyond the headland,
where the storm grew,
across your folded hands,
on those days most miserly.

Asking (or never failed to, at least once),
when known here, as you pretended,
that last Sunday of our lives. Is it real again?
Have you rubbed your eyes for nothing?

I wouldn't ask again if I were you,
too soon, my love, and yet so unable.
Where the tracks end, that is where
my steps then took me, *too soon a-day*,
furiously here, and then down again.
Lost forever, they do say.

Your head in my hands.
A matter of infolding,
nothing more than that
on any afternoon such as this one.
Have you not agreed?
Did we not take each other there
so soon, after all that had happened?

Entflieht

Death hurries us away.
Nothing to be claimed or thwarted.
I was never a part of it, unlike you,
with your arm projected to unseal.

I am not worthy.

The drums have rolled away
to reveal realms
of such blessedness.
Climb the stairs again!
Such stalwarts!
Such beginnings!

Funf Lieder

1.

The children are here with us,
as if stepping by, and then away.
Fly with them.
Be not unseemly –
as you might once have conjured.

2.

Awkward moments of such startlement!
You were not at all as promised.
I took it upon myself forever,
and more as we huddled together,
two at their gentle play,
in that gilded corridor –
before the war swallowed us –
with its oh so loving gestures.
Why such bruised skies though?

3.

Never to be stolen.
Never to be known at all.
You were no more than a gesture to me, idly blowing.
Would that I could have had you then,
would that I might have been framed
by the pleading of your window…

4.

Or not, if the time removes
all evidence to the contrary.
You stole me away,
and I was a privy to all your sanctity.
Who can deny it? I would have. Then.
I shall do it now, surely.

The horse has reared again.
Or nothing else must matter.
Latest day of all,
with spatterings of bright paint
on the balcony, blues, greens, yellows,
before your presence and mine.

That is all there is to it.
An inkling of something again.
Who could have said, if asked quickly?
Who would have told me?
Was it then an anchoring
in a range of perplexities?

Funf Satze fur Streichquartett

1.

Thwartings and sparrings.
Savage thrusts of more than breath.
See as far as you are able.
I took the scurryings with me in a bundle and ran.
And you? Would you chop the air freely?
Run then.

Judge for yourself all that matters! I hollered after.
There is just the one of me, *solus*,
and admittedly a touch lonely,
except when the fire combusts
and draws me to it,
in the drawing room again (needless to say),
with your matchless friend.

Pink with every breath.
Challenge me. Go to it!
I shall slide sylph-like sideways,
past you and on…
And, as I said, there is much to be gained
by running pell-mell across this grass,
arms furiously swinging.

We cavort. We hesitate,
we sometime fast friends.
I have never known you.
The gulp of our past
is all there is to it.

2.

Oh crossly shed in halves or quarters!
Who might have guessed?
Who could have told against us?
Such surreptitious meanderings and moilings…

3.

Caught in love's brazen net!

4.

How much was ever to be said?
The door scratches at our memories,
would you not say,
if not gone from me?

5.

Is it to take it all,
dragging it along,
from here to there, slowly?
Why this world so passing weary?
You know as much
as there is to be known.
You would have told.
You would have come clean
over a folded white napkin.
In the end I had to beg for you to leave.
Only the corner, with its light on.

Sechs Stucke fur grosses Orchestra

In the beginning, a small sputter.
Was there to be raging soon after?
Did you lie on a bed and wonder?
Flesh peeled away, merciless.
The thunder being itself a declaration.
Of mood? Of love? Of nothing?
On which branch?
And from which broken window?

That drabble of leaves.
The drabble remembers.
A gong calls, reaches and pleads.
I myself know nothing
when morning starts up again.
The patience to be had
takes its leave all of a sudden.

Head toil. Hand toil.
Foot drag and slow menace.
Much from little –
that is how we all said it.
A trip wire to be inching along
as a mark of no particular favour.
Come back when you are ready.
Gang, leave me!

The cautious creep of any Sunday.
No one carries more, believe me,
when I speak of the burden
of a life well lived forever after…
Or perhaps you have forgotten more
than I ever dreamed that you would –
if there is to be nothing
here for the asking…

Compensate for this a little.
When a table shows, sit beside it,

legs drawn tight together.
There will be much of you
to be remembered for,
daily or nightly…

Der Todesfall die Anton Webern

The death was terrible,
a kind of humiliation.
Friendly fire!
Except that,
to so many by then,
he was unfriendly,
being an Austrian.

He had stepped out into the dark
to smoke a precious cigar,
too precious for a single lifetime,
for this composer of mischance
and fragmentation,

a small, shy man
who owned his own thoughts,
and the tip of whose cigar
was glowing out there in the dark
on the porch of his son-in-law's house,
that dealer in contraband,

which was why the Americans had come after him,
and why they waited, close to the house,
to impose their night-hours' curfew
of which Webern, having known so little
of his journey, of how they had even made it this far,
carrying everything that was theirs about them,
feeling stricken, anxious and bewildered,
knew nothing.

Three bullets hit him,
three bullets did for him.
He fell where he had stood,
being then nothing,
at that moment of death's
sudden and most startling illumination,
being by then nothing but the anxiety,
the fever, the breathless onrush
of his music.

Streichtrio, Op. 20

1.

Not seen over there
when I asked you for retribution,
not yours, not mine, or ever.

Be damned to it all, you replied,
and then the wolves came leaping after,
pack animals beloved and scorned by so many.

Are you still with me?
Have I taken you all,
with these bundles about us?

It is always out and back,
with nothing to be said between except this,
and you have no wish to be a part of it.

Be damned to you then.
Be damned to all of you.

2.

High stakes – or wasted completely.
I took you there,
at which point you disowned me.
There is nothing but pitifully little,
only so much to be spoken of,
which is why I sit you down to question,
and then quickly toss aside
the least matter, if you are unable.

Why replace what has been completed?
Has there been much pleasure hereabouts?
Have we seen the tides come in again,
when evening saddens,
and we make our usual play together –
even if that were possible?
Were you with me or against me?

I plucked one clean out of its socket
and waited for new growth to stir
within those days still available to us,
nonsense speech for nonsense hours
of waiting and extreme foreboding.
My love, I say this to you today
even as it runs away from us:
it is all tantamount to guessing.

Symphonie, Op.21

Open, skies, after all is finished!
Make your grand flourishes,
declamations or what have you.
I want no part of it,
being a hole-in-corner sort of fellow.

Be big with us – or smallest to view.
I come and I arrest it all.
So much is to be done with so little,
even as the last iceberg melts away
and slowly, coyly vanishes from amongst us.

Bletherings from every tower!
Chippings and re-surfacings!
Slatherings across and re-appointments!
Would you ever say
that you had really known me?
Meanwhile, I wave to you
in a mood of scarcely suppressed frenzy,
eager as any gruff felon,
from across these lulling waters…

The dark is never quite upon us.
Daylight is a welter
of chance percussionings.
Meanwhile you still sing up there in your attic,
plaintive, wholly remarkable
to catch me back and tame me
to the tightest chordal structure
of your ancient-as-days pianoforte.

Out and in, and out and in,
that is always the message,
the cold, the heat,
the chance, prevailing winds of change
ever snooping upon us.

What is it to stalk or to plod?
Would you choose either
in preference to
any new day's chance blather?
Hear it all around,
or clasp it to you!
No freezing mist has ever quite enveloped you
when you had a mind to be curt and dismissive.

Roaring back and up,
the stalks are back, with all their menacings.
Let us call it the howl of nature
from behind, say, any wall,
where there is always a precipice
from which we must stand to observe
the random cardsharps at practice
in the lushness of our valleys.
I would take it all,
were I ever asked (as I am).
I would abandon nothing.
I would drive the spade deep, deep, deep
until I struck rock.

Quartett, Op. 22

Not the laughter proposed yesterday
for the nonce, or forever.
Pick it apart, deftly.
I still have it now.
Take. Eat. Quickly.
You squeeze me.
Here are the droplets.
Chance encounters.
Rocks falling in all their menace.
And still so unencumbered.

Upturned for my sake, surely?
The carriage in the hall,
once again, wholly mistaken,
when your arm grew to a size
to lift us, ever onward.
Yours or mine? I ask.
No one here for the speaking.

My love unrestrained,
shared unreliably,
not quite as far as this end
to all our grieving.
Was there ever majesty
in life's minutiae?
Your breathless state,
still and forever asking.

Let it leak out
and keep on running
until day's end,
snipped for any quick conclusion.
Audible and a chance to waken,
with threads running through so smartly.
Who would have foretold all this
when you were never here for the asking?

I chop and I change.
We wheel around again,
cosmically inclined,
and not a little bewildered,
marionettes on their folded poles,
fallen silent or dead,
or spoken for again,
as any might have foretold,
being wizards by profession
in any coming kingdom.

Crossed again! All mangled
and into the mincer!
You jest about so much,
raising your legs so high –
this high, in fact –
when you skip.

All's told, soonest forgiven
to any whispered acrobat.
Lacks for much then.
Or perhaps fired up
as any new-sprung felon,
leaning exaggeratedly, this way and that,
looking out for crossed swords in the gap.
Believe this? Or anything.

Konzert, Op. 24

Called to the spire, and then again,
on such a morning!
You took me back.
You spirited me.
The odds were all against
this kind of confusion, surely.

Catch as catch can
in the gap between this day and that,
ever more widely yawning.
I could not have said
what I had said to you
when such days came between.
Are you my bet, my stool,
my Betty has-and-has-not?
I for one have laid a wager on it.

Mingling apart and between
as the voices must tell us,
those shrill, high appointments,
all bird song, soon to be unravelled.
Melody is slathered over,
much of it silent and almost piteous
or as you would rasp when you
were too fearful to say it.

I admit something. Part the stalks
and let the wind sigh through.
The tree still hangs in the wind
for just as long as it has the patience
to be remembered or conjured
by pen, brush or crayon.

It is always to be said again,
and never too often,
there is so little boredom
in our minutes, hours, days of
consequential repetition.

Here is a quick unlocking
on to a window
where the dancers still gather
in fear and expectation.
I would not have this so.
I would not have you speak of it
if instead you may walk end to end
and measure the outcome
of all these actions.

Points all again!
And to the minute!
Laughter quite as much as is needed.
Or you may fall on your face
and gather the earth
into your cheeks until they swell
into the full stride of much buffoonery.
Let it go until it is beyond endurance.
Let it all arise now and frighten the tellers.

Streichquartett, Op. 28

Thrust out and beyond,
and then turn to face me
as if innocent as any snatch of bird song.
I have asked for nothing.
I never pledged myself to this moment
with its shrilly insistent rising.

Layer upon layer,
until soon we break through
and into the cross of new morning,
where all the savages are still
soundly sleeping in all their gaudy.
Cast nothing away,
least of all this long flight of millstones.

Is this for the taking?
Would you have the boy carry more
and yet more buckets of water until
his arms become numb and shrivelled?
Is it of myself that I am speaking?
All within the scope of such testiness.

How can it be, this listening?
With all clothes quickly removed?
And these gestures of such helplessness?
And no walk that is not unending
when the advice is of the kind
so readily to be given?

I have asked you.
I have asked you.
I have asked you.

And still you have not responded.

Five Movements for String Quartet

Rascality on the rise
in the waking up, yes, of days galore!
Had so much ever been so threadbare?
I would say not, having wielded a hammer
for its sureness of touch
on this breathless morning,
so soon lost, so soon gone,
of her most brilliant annunciation.

You crossed us again,
you stole it, and then you burned it –
for all of us, surely. Or if not, not.
Least of all *then*, and let me expatiate now,
much of this is not so readily mistaken,
not to such an extent that I cannot undo you,
were you even to ask such a thing of me,
which you may not, having been all that you have been –
I say as much, being myself scantily attentive.

Punctuate now, quickly – or rob the very life of me,
gut-wrenching, and now gutless.
Divide the garment between the several of you,
if – and this indeed is crutch or crux –
as much of this as is true
proves to be so, meddler minor.

Out of control, and then in the siding, idling,
an old man to be spoken of,
drab as any other, nursing his cough.
I catch sight of you, and then I let you go.
Such mufflings and back-row shufflings
and fierce abrasions of conscience!
Had you asked before?
Might you have dared?
Lothario took two steps forward
and tripped on his own shadow,
the chump on behalf of us all,

periwinkle in hedgerow,
were it to be spoken of thusly.

I have mined those seams daily,
and now look at me!
A wanton in all its glory,
cloak flung across shoulders,
at such moments, hours, of bewitchment,
the full panoply indeed –
and without a stitch of crossness!

Are we to be here then once again
when so much is lost to view,
so much has faded to sadness?
You took me back slowly,
though I remember nothing of it,
having given myself away that morning.
What cuts through now?
Who pretends to see with eyes fast shut
against the guttering of this roof?
It is not up there again.
It has all been removed,
and you have made an exception of the truth,
you tell me, letting the spool unwind
until my eyesight blurs
with the sheer good humour of it all
for once in my life.

Asperities, and the quick, scuttling
shot of the needle. Whoa now!
No one gave the order to rein in,
no one was even paying attention
when the landscape stopped and changed,
stripped of all its physical features
in an instant of sheer uproariousness
at which we were never quite present,
being soundly asleep
in the sands of eternity.

Are you an *habitué* of dunes?
I would call myself a make-weight,
something off to the side,
of abiding muscularity indeed, at those
high moments of dreaming or scheming.
Choose which. You are the arbiter
of souls and every other variant, it seems,
of modish soulfulness
as we have all come to know it.

Not across the bay in one leap.
Nothing happens in that way.
No light fends for itself,
and especially not when night
and all its mundane ramifications
threatens to undo us.
So much is mere pretence at wakefulness,
so much is idle bluffing of the sort
to be found in novels, soon shredded
by wind, rain and the general day's malarkey.

Does not coarseness
give us all that we need
for this long day's journey?
Would you not agree
when I invite you to come running,
fleet and light on your feet as a spirit
never wholly credible
in this world or wherever?

I can ask you twice at the most.
At the utmost, pardon.
To persist is so tiresome.
You must agree.
The blethering,
full of cheerful inanities,
persists, persists, persists
until dawn and then after.

Drei Kleine Stucke, Op. 11

Forced to act,
the removal of all pain
too readily, and then back,
or mine to be had,
but only in the instant.

Those are the sharps,
razor-fine, well-tempered,
upon which I must insist,
yet always in your forever idling presence,
with its kindly and so lulling dreamscape.

Did the voices call again
since last September, gaining?
I ask for nothing – or just as much.
I simply put it out there and watch,
idle, dumb, expectant,
in fact, much as I have always been.

So stand fast again, and be ready.
Let not talk come between
or any such idle gestures
when you call me back.
Whose deed anyway?
whose finer point of it,
yet always so makeshift?

Streichtrio, Op. 20

Could it be said all over again,
as if for the first time?
Had you even asked for an answer?
There were guards beside the bridge,
totemic though listless,
so much added enchantment
within the context of any river.

Loss is a calculable set,
when you all run after,
wailing and calling.
Not to the many.
Those few have always lost.
Too soon. Too hopeless.
Too helpless perhaps.
They always plead
before daintily skipping off.

I trace my blandishments
with a finger, ever wavering,
as do you, in the darkness of the closet
where the books all live, so quietly,
and the small talk too, inflammatory.
Of such is the chance encounter.

Health snatched her back.
Dissolution was nothing
but a chance proposal
on some Parisian stairwell
known to too few
on any summer's day
so passing sultry,

where you leant and you sighed
and then, of a sudden, remembered
all there was to be done
for just the two of us,
and then perhaps again,
craving your pardon, madam.

Have you loosened all the ties at last?
In the interim, count yourselves lucky.
The carriages shuttle in and out,
mind-numbing as ever –
or auguries of misfortune.
I wait here in a mood of…
extreme hesitation.

No gesture works for me
beneath the uncommon gloom
of such a cloudscape as this one.
The hand rises and then falls again,
unfailing in its insistence.
Why such loss of confidence
on a Thursday of all days,
that crown jewel of a yesterday
cherished by so many?

This much can be said at least:
there has been much shredding,
after which comes a loss of faith
for in excess of a century,
through which we all sleep happily.
Were I to ask again,
would the door respond
in its inimitable fashion?

That tap, tap, tap is nothing but
the past reporting on its whereabouts,
showing cheerfulness in the face
of uncommon adversity,
too late now to beg pardon.
Yours or mine though?
Who would be so bold
as to opt for condemnation?
We are who we are.

The same bags are still humped in the corridor,
there, always for the asking..

… As it could be.
Or were it to be made to seem.
In the days of interim expenditure,
too lacklustre to be posited as a cry.

Streichquartett, Op. 28

Oh so soon struck out
before the moment welters or returns!
If it were ever to be said,
who lives here to deny,
and beyond all endeavour?
I would not have it.
I would not stand for it.
There is a pressure
almost beyond endurance,
which you share now with me, granted.

All boxes to be gathered, counted.
Excellence, if such a thing remained
in this lack-land of thirst,
and then again, not, if you could be
forced to take it,
against your better judgement.
I hesitate beside the door.
I receive, gladly,
such goodness as is offered me.

But then, you are not there to deny
all that you said to me, are you?
You are a mere child again,
a bottle to be sucked, squeezed until dry,
and then crammed without mercy
into this bottom corner.

The last was a random stroke of mischance
without promise of a future.
You stood upright,
with your measuring rod,
posturing to the least of us,
and, as ever, deceitful.
Are we to return there?

Might you deny entrance
when the sky yawned –
as it always did on that day?
I can countenance no such thing,
and I would challenge you
to take it away
without fear or favour.

You walked that day
as if no sea could challenge you.
It was an open and shut case.
There is much envy, granted.
What is to be done?
Several poles upright in the ground,
and ever keenly a-bristle,
make for an errant victory of sorts
as far as the moon and its
pretty consort are concerned.

Are you still pleading?
So little can be shredded at this juncture,
mine, yours or what have you.
No single remonstrance must take its cue
from your behaviour.
Are you the best ever to have been?
Or is this a pardonable exaggeration?

Nexus.
Low throw.
Bucket, empty.
The anger of wasps.

Was that how it all started
with a chance, snatched look behind the screen,
where you were bathing until doomsday?
Did they all love you then?
Or was it principally a question
of some kindly assassin
lulling you to sleep
beneath the water?

Variationem fur Orchester, Op. 30

Lest you forget this first stroke of the pen…
Would a supporting role suffice you?
I stalked for a little while
before the dark utterly consumed me.
But this was so soon after
the forest snatched us away,
night owls that we both were and are,
scheming and listless as our several futures.

How is it to be said more than once
when language takes its leave of us
as if wholly uncaring,
with its customary whistle of contempt?
Can it be more than mere guesswork
if love is never to come between,
mumbling its string of half-hearted pardons?

Did you clasp buffoonery to your chest just then
as I was walking down that lane, quiet and unfeeling?
I have caught you! I have netted you!
And then life, of a sudden, reduced itself
to this long bout of tremulousness
accompanied by a busy, off-stage buzz
of machinery in a workshop,
something that no one –
but no one – had ever quite expected.

Much is grosser than you could ever have imagined.
Let me repeat that again before you interrupt me.
I really want for nothing, you know,
not even a sideshow of such and such dimensions.
Can it, in summary, be breathlessness after all?
I would have taken it for something longer
and much more consequential.
There have been many blots in the copybook –
count them for yourself if you have the gall –

I mean, of course, the patience.

Khaki or knapsack reminiscences perhaps
as you drool in your bed again?
Pity me not for being such a creature
who is never not waiting.
Do you believe in corners,
have I ever asked you?
Did you swallow one whole
yesterday perhaps,
when all of recorded time,
all those tiresome thens
and nows and soons,
seemed to be against you?
I joke not! In fact, I take you very seriously,
and I shall do so all the more readily
when you prove yourself ripe for re-assembly.
Pencil that in for the day after yesterday.

I expect little more than you offer.
When you stepped off, all at once,
where exactly did you go to?
Did you by any chance
join this orchestra,
of which I too am a member?
If we were, say, to live together again,
how soon might we become acquainted?
So many questions to hang in the air,
and all past the asking,
past motion even
on a dry, still day such as this one…
Your breath is as good as
done with this morning.
Don't think I haven't noticed.
You were never one to emerge
fully realised from all this murk surrounding.

Why not let God account for something?
Who set it all in motion other than the two of us?
I am never beyond the reach of jesting.
Solemnity chose once to lock me out of
its finest mahogany closet.
Ever find yourself
in such a mood of fabrication?
And, were it ever to be the case in fact,
would you have the good grace
to tell me, truly?

Quintett in Einem Satz

Lording it over
in that exemplary fashion,
where you trusted no one
at any corner of your being.
Could you ever have spoken truly
and admitted to such a loss
on such a drear spring morning?

I take you for nothing but a habit.
You have never been wanting
in so many respects to be pitied,
and there is still breath a-many
and beyond, had you failed to notice.

Walk with speed and beyond me,
or hesitate for a little longer
until yesterday must overtake us,
with all its losses and confusions.
This is quite as much as
needs to be spoken of,
you child-bride of a junkie.

Clap hands until we all fall back
and welcome the inevitable
with its gush of watery strings
looming for the loss of nothing.
Had you asked and, if so,
had I even granted?

Or a little less perhaps?
You are out on a limb this morning,
naked and squirming,
with little else to be looked at
and precious few to attend to you.
Who would ever opt
for such a solution?

My life weighs yours in the balance.
We look until our eyes fall into
that customary desuetude, my darling,
prinking and pricking at the outer limits.
Who would want any of this?
Who could have begged for it?
Yes came the answer, and then again.

You so much wanted to be believed
when there was still such an
abundance of light to interrupt
your boldly insistent cravings,
my superhuman hero or heroine.
Cast it all away then.
The sea's maw as ever yawns open.

The threat has lifted.
Day has re-scrambled its alphabet
to all our advantages.
See far then, my ancient crony.
Make light and life of so much.
Hurry to that bench
on the boardwalk this morning
where so freshly now
the weather is springing,
and deposit all your tonnage of wishes
as if you were nothing but this,
and had never been otherwise.
This is how precious all of life
must surely become for us.

O concatenations!
Such fury of hell's mouth opening!
No, it is not that after all.
Call it instead any cinema's afternoon
in a small town in the country
where you doze over some scene,
politely flickering or fading,
of Punch pummelling his Judy at the beach.

Had we ever known such loveliness
this side of Paradise?
I ask you several times,
and still you do not respond promptly,
as if you sincerely believed me to be
wholly alive and more within you.

Dig a little deeper then.
Lift. Plunge, sink with all your might.
You are up to it. You are not yet offering
(how does one say it?):
apologies for this uncustomary absence.
What's with all this devilry then?
Are you costumed thus out of habit?

I would have chosen to make you and re-make you,
given that you are a water-soluble substance.
Climb aboard again this morning.
Make of it what you will
as you ramp and scramble,
each of us wholly disbelieving.
Not so, you commented, adding:
only this and none other.
Break us then into several unequal pieces.

Variatonem fur Orchester, Op. 30

It it some god who stalks abroad?
Or did you rasp at me with the best of intentions?
I caught you at the corner, peeking,
twin brazen bushels swinging.
Have at me then, or lie down in this ditch
as an emblem of helplessness.
Knock is the meaning of wood –
a sharp lesson from your schooldays perhaps
when everything gulped itself down
and then on into the eye of a periwinkle,
as if nothing were ever again to be true or false
in this world of new-fashioning.

Fast, impish fingerings
before you falter and scamper off
(stage left) if you are paying much attention.
Always yours for the doing!
Or mine if I am to be asked to intercede
at such a kingly moment as this one.
Truly there is nothing hereabouts,
not a single stone unturned too many,
and you are no one again,
much as I may regret
such a pronouncement.

Coloratura, my friend?
Was that your customary prediction?
I somehow felt that I knew it.
Or did she wing in from the side,
all yellow lampoonings?
I never made a final request.
I always doggedly hung back, arms akimbo,
being who I am and must surely be forever.

This is the last of it, you must fear.
Hold fast to the black lapels of that jacket!
No one asks you for more than this.
There is only so much that can be said –
unless you disagree with virtually everything.

The boat has splashed down on the water.
Those ducks, believe it or not, remain incurious.
As do we, needless to say.
Did you find that chance opening onto yesterday?
You did not? You verily surprise me.

Sechs Bagatellen fur Streichquartette, Op. 8

1.

Or this distaste for all other.
Would you have at me again?
Is there all but assurance?
Keep your chronicles open as June weather.

2.

On to the rest of it then.
With a livid countenance, surely,
and the spectacle of none returning,
and least of all said so by any.

3.

Atomised or precious,
and all so quickly rendered.
Was it an attack on truth after all?
Is this a device for listening?

4.

Slowly turned and then about,
or you have betrayed nothing
that is to be said all day
without refusal or any gainsaying.

5.

Crisply laid out
as a feather – or not otherwise.
Were you here to ever answer?
I speak for no one but you,
and then open this shell before sighing.
This is more than enough,
being the equal of all your pardon.

6.

Precious breath!
What a lacklustre accompaniment
to be seen or offered
when the day breaks in half again.

Funf Stucke fur Orchester, Op. 10

1.

God sped us away to an answer.
Cross as can be made to be
before the last chance utterance
surprised me more than any other.

2.

Partial answers come slowly,
as you pass me by, here or there,
and then nothing answers,
and we are left here, lonely.

3.

Not to be measured, please.
How did it happen so soon
when there was nothing but
one random call or another?
Did you take a reed and blow it?

4.

Nothing walks as we surely must
if the event seeps through the cracks.
Without assimilation of this kind or any other,
there is nothing to be spoken of, surely.
Or perhaps not, with the rattle so just,
and this after all being our final measure.

5.

Duly impassive, or perhaps
you came just as fast as ever,
and then spoke too harshly,
as you sometimes surely must.

6.

Who plays in this way?
Is there a corner to be reckoned with?
I doubt you. I doubt myself moreover.
A board strips itself of all ornament
or, at worst, you could simply ask it.

Drei kleine Stucke, Op.11

There is an interim measure.
There is a day without reason.
Any bagatelle could carry me.
Yours are the reasons for such idle speculation.

1.

Imbalance too soon spoken of or contended.
Or when your task collided – boof! – with space
of such and such dimensions.
Too much, all tolled, for any speculative hurry.

2.

Mental sparks across the floor
drizzled as any blanket.

Funf Lieder, Op. 3

1.

Opening out makes for a little
to be granted.
If it should ever be asked of me.

2.

Anchored in hope and futility?
Or your shade running after
to ask the impossible again.

3.

Take it now.
Make it all, permissible
as you account for
this sky's tall conjectures
or what you asked
for all this to be
when the ending promises
a resolution of our taking.

Could it not be so forever?

4.

Less and less of us hereabouts
anchored in futility
is all that we ask now,
foreboding when the wave flows over
and a sleight of comfort
masks the next near perfect opportunity.

5.

Axe or heft.
You are still accustomed
to all this tragic apportionment?
No is the answer
when that little assumes
emotion past all glory to be spoken of.
Would you make such a day of this then?

Sechs Stucke fur grosses orchester

1.

Whatsoever is in this surprise
of mine hereabouts
in all its futility,
and the pull and the push
of its urgent drabness,
to take and to take,
is again a fullness
of nothing at all, I beg of you,
uniquely insistent again
after all these lapses
of time and
this shocking spillage
of lost memories…

2.

You may have called,
you may have walked
several pretty
and very well chosen paces,

and then, well, thought better
of the chasm presented,
with its customary drama
begging a fall,

loosening a rib or two
all being forever upended,
or you perhaps slipped there instead
into all the talk of which

you have always been so capable.
Let me know, sidelong if need be,
when you have a moment,
or can ever speak truly.

3.
Or not if you asked?
Or not if the world once again
slipped through the cracks,
and those under-notes
were now too terrible in their multiples
to see through to the bottom?

Needless to say, I have not called recently.
You were not beside me
to do the walking, and so I
strode off to the South,
manfully, and wondered,
or wandered, meanderingly,
stroke after stroke,
foot-slap after foot-slap,

until nothing was clear,
and then your presence here
was once again
a bright aliveness within me,
with all victuals still to be eaten
and the deck swept clean of its sea mist
on such a bracing morning as this one.

Were you ever to know
that all this had happened?
Did they ever tell you
by thumping the floor
with such insistence?

Enter again, and be amused
by the sight of these rollings,
spread out or slathered
for all our favours,
because next off,
time willing or unwilling,
you may catch
and then perhaps hold, nothing.

Or did you ask a slightly different question?
I am amused by this wall,
which is why I touch it and marvel
because there is so little
now to be broken,
and you have asked, surely,
the very last question.

4.

I said, finally, nothing,
which was a response to all the action,
and a drive perhaps to be different.

Hills rise, and streams wander at will
where the hazels nod benignly,
and so little else is ever to be spoken of

until you arrive to freshen the surface
with your bluster, and all springs up as if
nothing had ever been forgotten,
neither the pleading nor the getting.

Had there been much before the ending?
All was forever doubting,
and who can deny it

when wanton comes the spring
and then the petty vexations of summer
and those charmless bletherings after?

We strove a little once.
And then, as if on cue,
we stopped striving.

And there was none to notice.

Streichtrio, Op. 20

1.

Intermitted, you said,
before I fell back, howling-lonely,
and then you returned
where all the crossed particles
had vanished, without due warning.

Was it now? you were wondering
after it had all happened.
We gained on each other.
We had made a sorry mess
of this makeshift world, truly,
but then again quickly foregathered.

What is it to be here then?
Who could pose such a question
when night makes for a blanket,
a tissue of unknowing?
Perhaps then all is past and forgotten
in its stark semblance.

All corner tiles are fallen,
you have asked, so insistently,
again, again, again,
without a second's hesitation.
Were you as real then
as this tune hereabouts
that I am so brutally compelling?

Make it at last
from the beginning.
All told, it is quite a magnificence
in its gradual acceptance –
were you to be warned, that is,
and then ignored in your turn
before the past (and I have said this)
was still wholly forgotten.

2.

Lightness comes, and it jumps
in the way of all truth again.
When you asked for an answer,
I threw bells at your feet
with such unaccustomed violence,
and then stepped back, waiting.

My days are not here.
They have vanished into the aether.
Your crossed swords have sharpened.
Makeshift moments
are as unlike as any others.
Pile on all this waiting,
draw this thin thread
towards its unlikely conclusion.

Had you invited,
had you even proposed
an ending without arraignment,
I would have leaped or even pleaded.
You know that of me,
when all is forsaken without warning,
and the last are still left
so shrunken and hopeless.

Were there lights to be snuffed,
glad warnings to be flushed?
Hold yourself strong in the air.
Make for several amusements.
You delight me, hourly, daily,
when you pass and then behind,
leaving smeary traces of such heady action.

I would not have called forth
these landscapes of such boldness.
There was too little time to be had,
and the streets in all their steepness
had asked for nothing but venture.
I toiled. I spun back to the entrance,
giddy with anticipation.

Make it the last of all opportunities.
Your cranky spelling goes after,
seeking out loveless conclusions
of the kind long forgotten.
Not to be asked of me then,
or even quickly rescinded?
I would have said as much.
I would have chased you
as far as nowhere,
bearing the same stale peals of laughter.

Symphonie, Op. 21

1.

Let us lean and call forth,
one after another,
seeking out witnesses all,
before doom must fall, unhesitant.
You had not spoken
of such matters
to anyone but myself
on that day unlike any other.

2.

Lest we stretch out
and occasion a certain
lightsomeness of breath,
I would have it be known
that there is nothing else,
and you will be left with speech alone
in lieu of that missing companion.
Who knows when or whether?

3.

Have we then a miser in this pocket?
Did you enquire at the desk
for those reasons, if any?
Creak or whisper with two or three.
No one will stop you.
The hours are so tamed and incurious,
hopping on pogo sticks back to the entrance.

4.

This vale gives out happily
onto woodland of such abundance,
where the least little gift
ekes out the extravagance
of its pleasures to all and more,
whose presence hereabouts

is such a garland about our necks
before we even knew it.
Be gone then, and quickly,
before you step back to see
all that has been written about so giddily.
And take this no for an answer.

5.

Lack-land promises, with gulf *sprach* galore,
all falling away, and then succeeded
by promises of such and such duration:
I am yours to be known.
I am also yours to be abandoned.
You could never have asked as much.
You could not have pleaded.
Too sure were the boundaries,
too ominous the threat of futility.
So many men have already fallen.

Funf Canons nach lateinische

1.

What slopes yesterday,
with your bag free-swinging!
I climbed up to you, helpless,
and then the days re-appeared,
with monstrous billboards hanging.

2.

Were you there to greet me?
Is there nothing if not this again?
I asked, and then you repeated,
lackeying to the utmost.

3.

Everything is always so rapacious.
Is there still so little to be had or held?
Had you asked, I would have sowed.
So little now, with its muchness enfolded.

4.

At this point of waiting.
Much still to be eaten.
Did you brush it away, all told,
with such customary violence?

Quartett, Op.22

In all this thankfulness,
to steal in against you,
with the freedom to speak,
and all tabs so neatly turned over.

Was it a whistle – or a conclusion?
Asking is a departure
for movements and all their ascents,
too truly to be caught side-on.

Is it licence or the stolen
over which we dutifully anguish?
All to stand upright,
proving this corridor a happening situation.

Rock from side to side.
Believe me still here,
chancing in redness,
or so cheekily to be scuppered.

Konzert, Op. 24

1.

Well, whose dream!
Untoward scamperings daily –
or the mice to play outside
when all truth still struggles.

Were you wanting?
Or just here to be broken
across a ledge of basalt.
Nothing much else to be said.

Your wish was not over.
And seldom if ever accounted for.
Yours, I repeat, in all this loucheness,
beside, or next to, a wall of these dimensions.

Laurel stumbles, flickers.
Dance now into the coming penumbra.
Those who catch at us
will never accept all this goneness.

If ever to be known of us,
if ever to be spoken of truly,
always a holding back,
always a try and then failure.

Not pity, no such word,
nor the temptations attendant.
There is a roaring in the eaves.
Birds hop, and yet still flourish.

2.

Were you garlanded today
when the garden ignored your ankles?
I walked stately, I and all,
for the slow to be severed.

These miniature arrangements
ask for nothing but acceptance.
I would if I could. Your less
is still more than this chance occasion.

Or to be breathed out slowly
at every chance opportunity,
when here is as much as comes,
and you are still said to be waiting.

3.

What is this, to be had or otherwise?
Who jumped when the scenery fled?
Not in the call of things,
not in this waiting for the moment.

I said yes, and then again
I had waited for you, unwearying.
Once is never enough,
twice any vixen's spoiled nest.

Streichquartett, Op.28

1.
This is no answer.
The bells are so insistent
when the loom collapses,
and your minor take is so seldom.

2.
I and mine? To ask for so much?
From there hangs a table
in a room not yet approved.
Wait with patience for the outcome.

3.
Once or several, strivings all,
the slow grind of meagre opportunity
on a deck washed too soon.
As I then, never to be seen outside.

4.
Had you lied to me then?
This is a pixie-like engagement,
with all these flurries off to the side,
and consumerism run rampant.

5.
Your gait is wild.
Your edge is for the all and more.
Knock it back with a vengeance.
Chance a severe outcome. Only.

Variationem fur Klavier, Op. 27

1.

Are these the lost spice-lands?
No raucousness, smallest breathing.
You approached, always side on.
You did what you could, without wastage.

Are you a lack-land then?
Was that always the description?
There were crowds on the balcony.
You did sigh before you left.

I made it as nothing at all.
Here you are then, in that instant.
It has finished already.
All I am left with are these arms.

2.

Make it quick, if known at all.
Yours to blunder, mine to drift.
Exceptional fruit on a single bough.
How much ever to be said?

Not a gift nor a pardon.
Little to be seen again.
Whatness or howness, is it?
I thank you as much for being there.

3.

To speak very seldom,
and then not to look.
Choose, choose, choose, my friend.
It is all so tiresome.

Past whole world's bounty,
when bird-flight is as nothing.
To be believed is not credible.
You danced, wild, with all that fruit.

Is this a caper you asked for?
Are we here again or not?
Afternoon torpor, lest anxiety.
Or to scale a wall, a single leap.

And then to ask of us,
or to be aware again,
frightening every last ghost,
to be not much here or there.

Quintett in Einem Satz

I have gained on you now,
wherever our flight was lost,
or nothing to be hereabouts,
when this gone-ness is all plotted.

Instinct has gained on me.
There is a puzzle, a defiant swirl.
And you said as much again.
In short, I took it from you.

Were you the first to hear?
This reprise is convenient,
with a soul seated on its bench
and nothing to be said of it.

Would you have asked of me?
Did you take back the coin?
I made as much and more.
This is what nothing is for.

Could you call it a breath?
Did she enter this room without warning?
I want nothing of all of this.
I have chased myself back to the end,

where all truth was forfeited,
and I stared at the ring
which whirled about my head
and then, lone, began to sing

as we always sang,
arms akimbo, foot taps,
such jollity from nowhere
in the context of that meadow.

Did you hear as much?
Were you ever there?
Your apprehensive other self
would never have denied it.

This is the light shed for us,
all days still passing,
and quick returning to the end,
where you lie in bed, fasting.

And then all wakes to steadfastness,
and the ranks come surging
with nothing but mouths to feed
and your insistent reminder

that all this is surely true
and your weight is steady
and the ship is not yet drowned
and the kingdom is still ready

for your return to shore
anklets bright and blazing
with fishermen on your arm
and love at your elbow.

Is this your dearest dream?
Let us then speak of it
before the world's slow lull
makes it all impossible.

Too much the mire,
too much the welter,
when the pennies drop
and the hand of a brother

who stands to sing
and waits for you
to ask him back
before the moment's perishing.

Let it not come to this.
Be patient with these strings.
Too much the clutter here
before their grand opening.

I knew none of this,
and no one spoke of it.
There had been a fleeting glimpse
or perhaps a memory

before your return at last,
garlanded, though wretched,
lank hair again mirroring,
miserable in your skin.

Is this the truth of it?
Or is it overmuch?
I could have borne it then
if your own life had been.

Much or little to be said.
As much to be bearing.
Lift me up to the sky.
Let the light come breaking, tearing.

A Steady Downpour

A Steady Downpour

No single house could have contained it all.
I knew that even before I began to build,
or to gather up all the materials I would need
to create a dwelling such as the one I envisioned.

I recognised even then that it would be a futile endeavour,
and it was perhaps for that very reason
that I determined to create something
even more expansive than my most outlandish dreams.

Was I mad then to conceive of such a scheme?
Was I a fool to continue, even though I knew
it would be impossible to satisfy myself,
let alone you or you or anyone else?

And so I began, gathering bricks from odd heaps
stacked here and there about the city.
Who had abandoned them in this way in the first place?
Did not everyone need a secure dwelling place?

And so I began... but even before I had built the first wall,
I became exhausted and even disillusioned
by my palpable lack of strength.
If I could not build for myself, who then would build it for me?

All the others were so busy about their business,
far too busy to attend to my needs, had they even noticed.
What did I do then, in the end? Did I give up? Did I succeed?
Did I even try to complete the task I had set myself?

I am still asking myself these questions, to this day.
I lay one brick down upon another, quite steadily.
There is no end in sight, and perhaps there never will be.
And the rains still pour down steadily upon me.

On Not Missing You

Never let it be known
that I missed you
when I failed to miss you.
It was all a misunderstanding, you see.
You were not there with me.

All I could see
was one entire bedazzlement:
a sea-line so bright in its presence
that everything else hereabouts
could make no claims on me.

The Maddening Compulsion

I am finally compelled to write to you.
There is no other way to deal with you.
An absence can be too compelling.
Your knocking has been too insistent.

The interludes have yawned too widely.
An absence is a kind of promise.
Your presence was a curious absence,
a something I could never grasp at.

There is no other way to deal with you.
To write is all I know to do.
These days, these weeks, they count for nothing.
The interludes now yawn too widely.

I falter now. I grasp at nothing.
You name has vanished. Did you take it?
That name was always so compelling.
And soon enough I came to write it…

Spilled Light
for John-Francis

Let's begin with a single promise.
Easily kept. So easily broken.
To step out is to know too much.
To hold back is to disappoint.

This room is now a small, pent corner
where shadows gather for the comfort.
We out-lookers, we window-gazers,
see far too much to be acknowledged.

A screw takes comfort in the wood,
steadfast, cold and unforgiving.
That shaft of light you spilled for me,
I wash it back and forth for you.

Courage, Terror, Pardon

Did you say Courage?
I walked there once, between the shadows,
as evening gathered up its weaponry.
The world was such a nonchalance.

Did you say Terror?
I signed the form, in a small office,
then took the boat, as did the others.
So much was never to be spoken of.

Did you say Pardon?
I took her mouth, sealing its lips.
Her sweetness promised boundless favours
until they stopped, until it didn't.

The Old Artist and his Model

Every day has its clear instructions…
Stay perfectly still for a little longer.
Your hand, when it moves at all –
to scratch some damned itch
or what have you –
must not torment me.
Hold that pose.
A little less light if you please,
Mistress Snuffer off to the side!
You, girl, are an unconscionable fidget…

To stand on one leg
should not be too much to ask;
to pivot somewhat, and then to hold
and lean back,
hand firmly grasping the toes…
Now you have it! Now you have it!
This is why I throw good money at you.

The Death of God

He took me aside and he said:
make of yourself what you will.
I shall leave you now.
There is ample food in the larder,
and I have stopped all the bills.

He left me then, closing the door so quietly.
I looked around the room.
All was the same as it always had been,
and completely otherwise and strange.

I sat in his chair and spoke in his voice.
Moving back to my own, I nodded in agreement,
and then made some spaghetti,
for just the two of us once again.

I grew fat on double portions by and by,
fat enough to wear his suits, indoors and out,
without overmuch embarrassment.

Rivals in Portraiture

The woman said to the man:
raise me up, pose me, make something of me.
The man lifted the pen,
made various slashing strokes,
and then showed her the outcome.

I have been traduced, she told him, quietly,
as she in her turn took up the pen.
He posed for her: right leg thrust out,
chin steady and jutting, eyes fiercely attent.
She drew a careful circle
with a single dot in the middle,
so small that even she could barely see it.

The Nature of Seeming

If you ask me to explain it all to you,
it may take a minute or two longer.
There is no telling how slowly
the hours come and go.
There is no telling how much
you could have meant to me.

Now the moment of division has arrived,
and everything is heaped up in separate piles.
Yours is the more abundant, needless to say.
I can scarcely see you over it.
Noises of you emerge from time to time,
grunts, cheeps, odd burrowings.

I am for the most part asleep in these daylight hours,
resting from all the sufferings of bygone days.
I hear you come and go across the rooftops above me,
sometimes scampering, at other times hopping.
Is that not how it has always seemed?

Painting a Bucket of Nails

'I saw eternity the other night…'   *Henry Vaughan*

Take the nails, the handle and the rest of the bucket.
Lean it now against that fence post, in the sunlight.
There is no sunlight? The uplighter from the living room
may do just as well, having first located the extension cable.

Oils are good, pastels better, charcoal best of all,
because with charcoal you can so easily render
the starkness, the sheer, full-on austerity of objective life
as it comes and goes and comes, hourly, daily…

You tell me that sunlight throws down too much *pleasantness*
upon the scene to your taste, which is most particular, you say?
In which case, construct a canopy with some black scrim
thrown over to simulate a manufactured gloom.

Now, surely, you are ready – if you can ever be said to be ready,
with your facial spasms and your general surliness.
Are we to set to and *paint* this bucket full of gleaming nails
or not? And, if so, when? Eternity is only of a certain duration.

Mine is, at least. I saw it just the other night,
making something singular of me.

Darkness and Light

Out of Darkness and Light,
strange curdlings of the two,
we all emerge.

Which element is to dominate?
Or is one side forever to be black
and the other white,

as if we were all clowns
costumed and tricked out
for the Big Top,

mad tumblers,
white-mouthed yelpers,
ceaselessly running round and round,
urged on by the children
of this world
who would never wish us to stop

Violets

Violet

Just stand there and speak of love again.
We understood each other. Much else may never be known.
I caught you back at a moment's notice.
Yours is the signature on this letter.

At this window even now I prepare for you,
glass in hand, looking down into the garden.
After the rains, spring has returned,
and with it the smell of you. Violets.

Say something quite ridiculous again.
If you do that, I may gently push you.
Easy does it though. No spillage.
So much feels fragile hereabouts.

Missing Questions

Is this the question you always needed to ask?
And is this its moment?
So much has skipped away lightly in recent days.
So much has gone missing.

Were you always the woman I took you for?
Or had I misremembered some fundamental matter?
We took a bowl. We carried it out to the porch.
What exactly were we measuring?
This conservatory seemed just right,

chairs comfortable enough, with the side-trays…
Space enough to balance all that we needed…
And you within such easy reach of the sunlight.

The Snoopers

We both hated them coming,
the way they *snooped* when they looked about.
They may have lived in this house before.
That didn't mean they still owned it.

The best moment was easing her back into the overcoat,
the way she pushed her shoulders up – a mite coquettishly,
as if she wasn't a monster these days, so heavy
                    and so square of face,
as if some foolish part of her believed beauty endured.

He was a little better, we both said that.
Infirmities had cut him down to size.
He didn't even complain about the food any more.
In fact, he remained almost wholly and blessedly silent.

So Much

I caught you slack-faced and asleep one afternoon.
So much of you had left me.
I had to take a brisk walk, down to the weir,
and have a pint or two for equilibrium's sake.

How much was there, really? Did we ever ask?
Anybody falls so easily into the future,
especially when young and careless and foolish.
Doesn't that pretty well sum us up?

And then you blinked awake, smiled at me,
rubbed your eyes, jumped up quite briskly,
even kissed me on the cheek…
Maybe there was still so much of you.

The Miracle of Coffee

These days nothing ever really happens
because we make nothing happen.
Even the clock gets oppressive,
the way it refuses to accept everything's stopped.

A single robin gets our attention
because I've dug in one corner of the garden,
and it's found a worm to thrash about in its beak.
We laugh at that. Something about the sky feels
                a touch more open.

Coffee is still the same quiet ritual.
I bring it in, both cups, without blundering,
praying for new miracles of composure.
It comes, it comes, even in the raising of these cups.

The Old Voice

Your voice in the early days,
is that the same voice I still hear?
Or is it fuller now, noisier, more strident?
Right at the beginning then, did it seem to hesitate

before speaking, as if no one could be sure
they'd be the right words, in the right place,
and, similarly, you'd stand there, tentative and insecure.
Is that what so endeared you to me?
Now you stride ahead as I try to catch

the words you throw out as you accelerate,
and then wait for me to arrive alongside,
panting, gathering my breath, flush-faced…

Saying Names

I'm no more likely to forget your name
than I am to forget my own. Sidney.
Say it then after me, say it,
even if it's just for a game.

It's one you used to play, remember,
when we first met, or soon after.
It struck you as odd sounding, you told me,
like the whistle of a steam train

of the kind we watched at the station
as children, platform tickets in hand,
side by side with our parents.
What monstrous machines they seemed!

Knowing You

I never quite knew what it was that you knew.
I didn't need to. Your presence was enough for me,
the nature of that stillness when you looked about,
as if your eyes alone could calm the world.

Think of the days we walked out,
through the park, and then back down the lane,
so narrow I used to listen to your breathing,
so many delicate, quick breaths to get me going…

Now when you sleep in that chair, there's a rattle in the air,
as if some part of a machine's malfunctioning.
I pity you then when I look at you down there.
I feel like emptying out the tool box, doing some essential repairs.

Hero-Posturing

When we met, it was a new beginning for both of us.
Love's momentum kept us going for so long.
Everything seemed so hell-fire speedy, with all that laughter, revelry,
fumblings at the door to get the key in fast enough.

Now look at us, what we're reduced to finally,
walking in line, slow-paced, down this street,
barely looking up for fear of what might happen to our feet.
If I'd told you back then, you'd have given me
                your whiplash laugh.

Now it's flies have all the momentum hereabouts,
weaving round and round our heads with that maddening buzz.
I roll up this newspaper. I lunge out mightily,
hero-posturing as I always have

Slackening Back

This newspaper makes no sense any more.
The type dithers so much I can barely read.
So I give up, take a sip of coffee, sit back.
Needless to say, you're already asleep.

I look at you there. Your chest rises and falls
beneath that cardigan fully done up.
You look so peaceful, so brim full of love.
I want to reach out and kiss you, old love.

Then you wake up, flash me an angry look.
Who knocked just then? Did you get it?
There was no one, Violet. It was just a dream, love.
Oh you, say, oh, jawline slackening back into helplessness.

Helpless

We don't even want the visitors we had back then.
They're just a nuisance now, a pain.
When they ask, we say: no, all of you, just stay away!
Well, we say that to each other, not wishing to give offence.

Why *not* give offence though? They're just circling,
waiting for the give-aways. What's to be done?
We've always had too much stuff,
and the more we bought, the more we craved –

three-piece suites, side tables, sets of this and that,
ornaments enough to fill up a truck.
It's all just junk to us now, we know that,
and we sit here amongst it all, feeling utterly helpless.

New Muscle

We trundle along as we always have.
You have the same old gripes. I fuss over books.
Too many books! you always say when you look
at the walls of this room. Have you read all this stuff?

I pull one out, hand it over. Just read that.
You cough. Too much dust! The floors are bowing…
You point to hairline cracks in the ceiling.
We call the Fire Brigade. It's not reassuring.

Now they're all gone, barring two or three.
Shakespeare. Browning. A Roman history.
Emperors were ruthless back then. I'm not like that.
Too late now to put on new muscle.

Two Chairs

Something's lost, more than just stuff.
We wait for it to happen. It never does.
It's not just rain like it used to be.
Even in good weather, nothing brightens up.

I look at you. You look back.
We have no presence any more. There's nothing left.
Routine now is what keeps us going,
in and out of this room, doors opening and closing.

Where did it all go? Could you say?
You don't even want to ask.
Nor me. I'm past the point of caring.
Here are our two chairs. Let's fall asleep in them.

Or Not

Some of what I said was true.
Goodness knows about all the rest.
We did so much splashing around with words.
I so much wanted to impress you.

You see, I was trying to shine for you,
make myself as tall as I could be,
and make you into the most that you could ever be.
Did we succeed for a while? Is that the truth?

I'm not sure any more. My judgement's gone.
We just float around these days, mumbling.
I pick up this cup and hand it over.
Sometimes it's full, brimming over. Or not.

Raising a Finger End

I've said all I wanted to say.
And you, have you quite finished too?
You opened your mouth just then, looked at me,
then slowly closed it again, looking away.

Bird flight is all I seem to see.
I follow them with my eye, even smile inwardly.
Do you do the same? Is the bird bath empty?
We don't even care any more. We don't go to see.

Too late or too early, it's all the same really.
Everything's at rest, everything's shut down.
I tinkle this spoon in the saucer for the sake of it.
You raise a finger end. You wag it from side to side.

Officially

I'm signing my name for your sake.
Who else would I do it for?
The hand trembles a little. I try to keep it steady
for your sake, Violet.

This form is instead of you, we know that,
as does the man sitting opposite.
He takes it from me, unsmilingly.
He's practised at the grave nod.

This is not the only form I'm dealing with.
They're all up in the air, wafting from side to side
like birds in flight, all about to land,
though not here. At least somewhere.

All There Is To Be Said

Have you or haven't you?
Did you – or did you not?
I'm sick of all these unanswerable questions.
What are we asking them for?

All the sums have been done, to my understanding,
books all closed, doors locked.
We've even walked away from this house
like two fond familiar ghosts.

And now we're wandering the lanes hereabouts,
in company with children's chatter, the odd horse and cart.
You see, we're nowhere any more,
and that's all there is to be said.

More Than Enough

On this day like any other,
I look out at you from the back window,
walking back and forth, steadily,
fine arc spilling from the watering can.

The rhythm's steady. It goes on. It goes on,
after the kettle's boiled, after the tea's made,
so I have to rap on the window, gesture down.
Just then, cocked angle or not, the water runs out.

To stand beside you, cups raised, sipping,
looking out and saying nothing,
that was more than enough for me.
That is more than enough for me, Violet.

The Best of Us

I have sought no promises of the dead.
Let them die as they always lived,
ripe and ready unto themselves,
timelessly selfish souls.

I have asked no questions of our king.
To strut back and forth is his way,
withholding, dispensing his wave
on dreary days such as today.

I have asked for no special gifts.
You give what you can or must,
niggardly, open-handed or not.
The best of us tarnish, rust.

Reeds in the Wind

Reeds in the Wind

What did you know of all of this?
Seldom much.
Shufflings in the alley,
smashings of glass,
cries in the night, heartfelt,
a few random shots,
And then silence,
the long silence of the aftermath.

What did you say of any of this?
Almost nothing.
A few words, vague, embarrassed,
describing…well, not very much –
how a man walked over to her, them,
exchanged a few words, unheard,
then scuttled back.

How do you live with yourself these days?
Make do and mend.
Out to the shops, then back again,
as little as one might need,
with few words to be shared
amongst those still left,
back-turners all, sometime friends,
reeds gracelessly bending in the wind

The Sweet Play of Fabric

How was it then?
Not quite as much
as I might have wished.
She spent too little time here.
All I have now is this dress.

Adequate consolation then!
When memories fade,
fabric run between the finger ends,
just plays and plays…

Before You Fade

When the days are limitless,
nights brief, and so cool in their sweetness,
it is then that I see you
once again entering
in by the window
when the others all sleep…

Wait! I say, as you approach,
liking to see you there,
one leg still raised,
ever the eager beast,

I want to hold you as I remember
before you fade
and I am old,
and the nights have grown
long and cold.

Facing the Sea
for Nick and Marietta

You left me for reasons known only to yourself.
Inconsolable, I cried over your picture until Tuesday.
Then I left the house, complexion unblemished,
saying to myself: the sea will understand,
the sea is larger and wider than all our tragedies.

You left me without a word, taking so little.
Even your sandals lay splayed here beside the bed,
awkward, sweat-soaked, sand-impregnated.
I could not bear to touch them for days.
Now I have thrown them across the shingle.

I do think of you there, facing the sea,
dandling those sandals, wistful, hopeless.
But not for long, I do hope, my dear sis.
You know there are worlds far beyond me.
You know your own strengths as a swimmer.

Paris! Paris!

The Rue de Rivoli stretched from end to end!
Are we there again?
Is that an almighty fanfare
of all the days of our happiness
that I can see in front of me?
Or is it still this fog-choked London garden?

I don't count any more, my darling.
The tools have all left me.
I was never any good at counting, you may remember.
Call it helplessness, having arrived now at this corner
where the traffic lights wink so brazenly down at me
in all my wormy smallness…

How dare they do such a thing,
knowing the age that I am?
Should that cause me to look down at myself too as I lie here,
waiting for entire worlds to happen again, fool that I am?
I am not here to be pitied, you know, or I would tell you.
I lie here so long these days. There is no end to all this lying.
Sometimes, for a bit of variety, I thrash about or turn.
There is limited scope for real adventure.

We walked there, arm in arm,
in the direction of the Place de La Bastille, I recall,
past the statue of Beaumarchais,
that puffed up old posturer in his bronze frock coat.
You on the other hand were lovely, the smell of you, that is.
You leant into me, but gently,
as if I were so delicate and frangible.

You were also smoking something
absolutely filthy and irredeemably French.
I had to find it in my heart to forgive you.

You absolutely refused to be forgiven, you told me,
and so we left it. We let it all drift away,
it being the afternoon that it was, so still and so fuggy with heat.

We both longed to see the river again,
and so I said to you: *let us go then you and I*,
and we took the turn by Samaritaine, walking so slowly
because there was no reason on earth to hurry.
And there is still no reason on earth to hurry.
Why were you angry that day?
Why were you so often angry with me?
I have been a specialist in self-effacement.
I make it sound like a profession.
The fact is that I don't even believe myself when I say it.

I do not even know I am there now again,
why I have conceived of such an outcome,
except for the old longing. It pulls at me. It pulls at me,
everything that I see now again so vividly,
everything that I shall never see again
because my limbs are no longer prompt to obey.

On that same afternoon, we had walked down from the Butte.
Such energy we had in those days!
We stopped over in the park, Rue Burc
(that little uphill turn up from Rue des Abbesses),
where the children ran round and round, screaming,
learning to be outdoors unruly,
and you read, head lowered, in order to be alone
              with your book again.

You were always alone with your book again
and you could never tell me about it because it was always poetry
and poetry, you always told me,
is not to be described in so many words
because it is the setting forth of feelings as intangible
as one dab of colour laid upon another.
There is nothing to be said about such a thing, you always told me.
It enters in, inveigling, side-on,

like the faintest waft of another being.

Speaking of feelings, I open and close my hands regularly
in order to stimulate the circulation of the blood these days.
It is important not to let the feelings die away from the fingers.
It is important to stimulate the circulation, which I always do,
at least two or three times a day, being an obedient little girl
of a tired old woman..

When I grew a little tearful on that day, you closed the book,
having carefully marked the page with your bookmark,
and then took my hand, quite firmly,
as if to chastise me or at least to bring me to heel,
make me see some sense for a change.

Should we go then? you said, looking away
to the gate of the park, which had just squealed open
to let in yet another pushchair with its harried mother
and one or perhaps even two babies,
with another child going ahead, jumping, running…

I so often felt like a complete fool,
the way I let my feelings run away with me,
as if I were a child hurtling downhill on roller skates, screaming.
What a fool I so often was!

***

Later on they close the blinds, which means the blanking out
of the remainder of the day, which I do not like
because I long to observe every last soft fragment of its waning,
as night comes on, threatening to snatch it away from me.
Night is such an old misery, so joyless in its antics.

It is a little like that very last sip of tea from the cup,
cherishing it, savouring it, feeling the warmth in
        the tips of the fingers…
They laugh at me when they reach out. I pull it back, defiantly.
It is quite a little ritual, my games-playing with the tea cup.
The trolley ladies all love me for it. They expect it of me.
I have even come to expect it of myself.

After the light has gone, there is nothing else to keep me cheerful.
I am alone with myself. You are not here to console me.
You do not wake me up by accident in the middle of the night
as you always used to do.
I do not get cross with you for doing so all over again.
I am sick at heart of getting cross with you.
And yet what is there to do when you disturb my sleep,
and so much anger wells up inside me?
Would it not be even worse to ignore it?

All those problems have gone away of course,
you were a nuisance for no more than half my lifetime, darling,
and I suppose I should be glad of it, to be rid of all my burdens.
But I am not glad, not at all, for of what else does life consist
but burdens, burdens linking hand with burdens?
That is why I have grown so stooped and so old,
I recognise that now, because I lifted so much day after day,
things tangible and things intangible, and every one a nuisance.

And yet there was that one night, though I say it myself,
in Rue André Gill, which was unlike any other.
Why were we not sleeping?
What had caused us to open the windows
and throw back the shutters in order to let
in the roar of the boulevard,
the mad-cap world of Place Pigalle?
Such beauteous trannies were posed on the street corners!

Had we not been playing Kathleen Ferrier
on the gramophone,
absorbing all the sweet, grave solemnity
of *St Matthew's Passion*, as the children slept soundly
in the back bedroom,
and we sat around the table beside the window,
tearing at the last few remnants
of our second or third baguette,
dicing our cheeses, the tiny goat's, the bigger sheep's,
into ever smaller slivers
so that the evening's ritual of the bread and the cheese,

the red wine, the bread and the cheese,
would never quite stop happening
when it happened?

Two men came running,
one chasing after the other.
There was a glint of something brandished in the air.
It was so dark now down there.
Round and round the statue of André Gill they ran,
as if it were some children's game they were playing,
and no sooner had they arrived beneath our window
than they were running off again, back where they had come,
turning down the Rue des Martyrs,
with you leaning out, and shouting hoarsely after them?

Did we sleep much that night?
Did we not watch, as if mesmerised,
lights washing back and forth
across the ceiling?
From where though?
And had there been murder, mayhem indeed
after they left us?
Was one of them lying in his own blood
outside the Moulin Rouge?
We were never to know.
Next morning, the tourist crowds
were walking back and forth
over stains of blood, gum or vomit,
who would ever know?
Who could ever know?
The street cleaners,
those green men swinging their brooms,
were always so busy at it…

And I too am a little sick today.
Something has risen up in my throat.
Nausea hangs around me like an unwelcome stranger.
I feel disinclined to speak or to move at all.

To move, even to shift my hips from side to side
for the sake of greater comfort, makes matters worse.
And so I lie here perfectly still, head turned up to the window,
from where I can see the cranes reaching up
like a quiver of long arrows pouring,
on the diagonal, up into the sky,
those cranes with their red lights at the tip
to stop them being invisible to the helicopter pilots
with their expensive passengers.

We do not want another tragedy.
There have been tragedies enough and to spare.
I would not call my own life one of those tragedies.
That would be to exaggerate.
That would be to wallow in self-pity.
My mother, bless her soul, would caution me against it
and I, for once in my life, would be inclined to listen to her,
were she to be alive, which she is not.

There were no tragedies in Paris.
There was only ever loveliness there,
and this in spite of the fact that we had such small children
to see to. How we longed for them to fall asleep!
Any sleep would do! Any sleep was blissful,
and especially the afternoon's, which felt like a gift.
As soon as the last small voice –
well, there were only two, let us not exaggerate –
had fallen silent, we would sink into a chair
and sleep. There would be street voices drifting up
half-heard, melodious, quite distant in their querulousness.
We would both attend and not attend.
We would hear only as much as pleased us.
That is where I live now, habitually.
I make an effort to remain there
through all these nights and days.
No one prevents me.
They are all so understanding.
I spread out my postcards
of my favourite places on this bedside table –

Sainte Chapelle, Rue Monsieur Le Prince,
Jardins du Luxembourg, Musée Marmottan,
and the Orangerie most of all
with the great hush of that Monet.
I slip into the lily pond,
in the penumbra of that long room,
and I am utterly contented to be alone
where it is all so hushed and still.
And I do not ask you to be with me, darling.

Voicing

I am to be led back to the beginning.
This is no shock to me. It is how it has always been.
Certain words offer themselves, nothing special.
I pick about, as if amongst gravel, seeking a jewel…

Nothing comes. Nothing sings out.
Let me then resort to the humdrum crowd,
amongst which I have lived time out of mind,
outside any realm of perpetual surprise.

Now talk as you might to someone in particular,
an old friend, accustomed to your voice, to whom it is familiar.
Words will thread themselves into a pattern
pleasing enough perhaps for the duration…

Fishy Money

That fish on the hook
had money in its mouth,
money best deep-fried,
money best eaten whole,

money with a sheen to its skin,
money that will let you in
to worlds unfathomable,
and love, love, love to gorge on…

Tell me, Mister Fish,
why did you turn away
when I tried to take
your money away?

Why did you swim and swim,
with me swimming after,
and then drop it in the sea
for pirates to go after?

The Bell-Hop

Is this ugly boy waiting to be called?
His uniform is surely the colour of the lavatory door.
And yet the buttons, the epaulettes are so high-polished
that you would think he really cared
about the urgency of your call…
Did he not raise his head when the bell jangled,
drag on those ill-fitting gloves again (still the colour of suet),
and even seem about to push himself up from the knees?

But no, perhaps not.
Others can go first, the juniors, the eager ones,
his weary, absent look seems to say.
He has seen it all before,
all the misery of those long, ill-lit corridor days,
when grimaces turn to forced smiles
before the heaving of ponderous suitcases begins,
up ever steeper flights of gloom-struck stairs.

One Daughter to Another:
A Garland of Fourteen Poems
in Loving Memory

Our Favourite Tumbler

Was it you
who came through
here just now
in your unstoppable abundance,
cartwheeling through this garden?
risking all of our love for you,
you risk-taker you?

I saw you then
as I see you now,
light-stepping into
the tumble-dryer
as a tiny child,
on the turn-and-turn,
and the spin-and-spin,
so giddy with excitement
that there is nothing now
still to come
between you and everything…

The Measure

This is the measure of our love for you,
that we will carry you with us
along every road that we travel,
careful not to spill you,
and mindful to acknowledge
that the weight of you
is equal to all that
you have ever meant to us.

This is the measure of our love for you,
that we must listen to you
talking to us again
in that hectic and breathless way of yours,
your face full in our faces,
in all its brightness
and its desperate and terrible insistence.

This is the measure of our love for you,
that we will listen to you repeat over to us,
and then over again,
all that you must do, and where and when,
what you will need to buy to make it happen,
and all that you will need to consider
before making your decision
to descend into peacefulness at last
by leaving us forever.

Lips Sealed

The very last question I asked
you left unanswered.
I had said to you:
if, in your view, it surely must be,
what can I do to prevent it?

Would you not wish to
continue this conversation
by hauling up from the depths
the story of your misery,

so that we two
can ask what it has all meant,
and why oh why
it has come to this in the end?

I am still posing that question.
And your lips are still sealed against me.

Please

Can there be much still to be said?
Or have we said it all already
in every word the two of us could muster
on every day available to us?

There was always so much,
and you were always so ready
to share yourself with me,
to such an extent that I ask myself
how can I now make up
for all that you were to me?

Will others assemble, bit by bit,
the disparate parts of you?
Will there be a glance here, a grin there,
some outrageous gesture
that will in the end
summon up the whole of you?

Will you, in the end,
be standing in front of me again,
never having left me?
Please tell me.

A Different Story

There was a pause just then.
The world seemed
to stop breathing.
Voices fell silent.
The wind had slackened.

I looked into the room
where you had been standing.
Just moments ago
we had been talking.
I had not heard you leave.
You had not said
your goodbyes to me.
Your coat was on the table,
(well, half on and half off the table.)

I went to the window.
I stared at the day
in all its maturing.
Sunlight had given way to shadow.
In spite of the intersection below
being so familiar,
everything was now telling
a very different story.

The Trickster

Why did you wake me just then
to tell me you had left me?
Could you not have
left me soundly sleeping?
Would that not have been
the sort of kindness
usually shown to a friend?

Now I will never sleep again
because, frankly, I do not believe
A single word that you tell me.
It is all, frankly, wrong.
You are everywhere about me,
the smells of you, the looks of you,
the way you always
imposed yourself upon me
over so many days and so many years…

You have never not been here with me.
So why would you wake me now, so abruptly,
in order to tell me such bare-faced lies?
Why would you risk such a
precious friendship as ours
over such tomfooleries?
Would you want me to count you a trickster?

Counting the Minutes

You stole all the minutes I had left.
I had been counting them,
keeping them to myself,
Asking each one: is this enough?
Am I doing you justice?

And then you robbed me
of all powers of conversation
by stealing my minutes from me.
Now there is nothing more to be said.
My every last minute is yours for the reckoning:
what to do with it, and when,
whether our lives are ever to be shared again.

In the End

It has come to this in the end –
that you are leaving me.
I never asked you for favours.
You chose to share yourself with me.

And I readily accepted
because our fit was perfect.
We walked in step together.
You ended my sentences
when I was lost for words.

Now I shall be lost for words forever.
Why behave so harshly with me?
Had I offended you more than ever before?
Or had I never sufficiently loved you?

Your Jump

Was I listening just then
to a chorus of voices?
And was yours not amongst them,
no sooner there than gone?

Every street holds promise of you –
the way that girl rounds a corner,
running and running and running…
Can I ever keep up with you?

Or should I admit defeat,
say that you always outran me,
stepping too lightly for this world,
as, now, you jump, quickly, into the sky –

and then vanish.

Never Now Not

You took your leave of us then,
abandoning us here
to pick up the pieces.
It has been a loss like no other.
I knew that I would not,
could not, find you,
no matter where I looked,
nor how hard I scrabbled
amongst your boxes.

You had said the words to me.
You had whispered them even
when I was refusing to listen.
Yet still those words lingered.
No violent shaking of the head
has ever rid me of them.
The plain truth of it is this:
you will never now not be with me.

Before Cycling Off

Bicycle on shoulder,
You walked up to me,
and asked: are you ready?

For what? I replied.
For everything, you said,
staring at the road ahead.

How the cars seemed to terrify
that day by their speed,
their unstoppability!

For all that? I asked you.
You kissed me so violently
before cycling off.

Falling

You cannot have done what you did.
There is no separation between us.
I walked across to you just then.
We clashed pushchairs in the garden.

You cannot now be where you are.
We have all fallen into the water.
The man is filming us, over and over.
When will we ever stop laughing?

This day is not what it is.
There is no silence between the silences.
It is all voices, voices, voices.
You are always falling off the wall again.

What You Needed to Do

Bring your Brompton with you.
Or anything else
that you choose would do.
Everything by which
to remember you.

Or even that damp tissue
fallen from your pocket.
I wouldn't care.
I'd pick it up, keep it.

Your eye is bruised blue again.
There's a halo around it.
Let me touch it.
Here's some cream to heal it.
I'll massage it in for you.

Don't get on your bicycle too soon.
It's far too late already!
Not now. Not even tomorrow.
Linger here a little while longer.
I fear how you'll cycle away from me.
You were always so determined
to do what you needed to do.

Too Late for Comfort

At the next turn of the stair
you of all people were there,
pointing up to the landing,
and, of course, giggling.

Shush! you said.
You shush! I replied,
trying hard to stop laughing.
She's asleep in there! you added.
I know! I jibed.

And then you left me.
There was sunlight across the bed.
My eyes were open
to the day that came after.
I had woken too late for comfort.

Dear Bill

i.m. William Carlos Williams

I had a dream about Bill the other night. Bill is a friend of sorts. It has been that way for many years. It is not a relationship involving physical intimacy – he has been dead for many years. In this dream he is rising up from his seat, and reaching towards the bookcase which seems to tower over, and even to lean down towards him, as if to give some necessary assistance. His arm, as it reaches out, trembles a little. It is a tremor of anger, I know that for a fact. What is he angry about? I can see how old and relatively weak he is. He has suffered many strokes, but still he forces himself to write. It is an absolute necessity. Life would be nothing without the prospect, the promise, of the next poem. To hammer down on the electric typewriter with one finger will do if that's all he can manage, and it often was, towards the end, which came in 1963.

My dream comes to me in the bedroom of a Spanish garden in Andalucia, before the sun rises above the distant peaks of the Sierra. This seems just about right. Bill had strong Spanish connections. His mother was Puerto Rican, and they translated Quevedo together, haltingly, because his mother was very old when they worked on that project… I am reading Bill again, his poetry, his novels, his essays, his letters, settling back into the rhythms of his writing, which I have not read seriously or at length for many years. My first books by Bill were acquired almost sixty yeas ago when something I could not quite define drew me to him, quite compulsively. Bill lived for most of his life in the small and unfashionable town of Rutherford in the unfashionable state of New Jersey, which begins on the northern shore of the Hudson River, just across the water from the pent and forever unsleeping razzle-dazzle of Manhattan. Two quite separate worlds, so physically close and yet so far apart. Bill lived in Manhattan for a while, but it did not suit him. New Jersey, that blue-collar state, was where he belonged, amongst the poor, working as a doctor life-long. The making of literature belonged to the wee wee hours.

When I open the shutters this morning, I look out onto a pepper tree where the local chameleons do their climbing…

Chameleon Avenue

This little spur of a gravel avenue
Leads you round the pepper tree.
It's a viewing place for chameleons, you see.

Look up through the leaves.
Try catching them at their games
Of hide and seek,

Long, twiggy legs extending so balletically
In their extreme slow-motion reach,
All-over green like new shoots,

Climbing up, up, up…
Show some patience now.
In fact, scarcely breathe…

What did Bill's life amount to? He was a frenetic human being, who squeezed at least two lives into one, doctor by day, poet by night. Fragments of poems demanding to be heard were always assailing him, often at the most inopportune of moments. He would jump up from the dining table of his relatively modest two-storey house in Ridge Road, Rutherford, New Jersey, when a line beckoned, and take the stairs up to his study, at speed, two at a time. These things came and went, precious jewels, shooting stars across the night sky, which vanished if you did not seize hold of them. As a young man, he was lean and feline.

Part of my job in this little book, is not exactly to write Bill back into existence, but to bring over something over his character and the quality of his work, to engage, through poems and fragments of prose, often set in and descriptive of this sequestered spot in Andalucia where I am currently living, in a bit of mimicry and appropriation of his manner, to bring him back to life for myself, in a way which will also throw some attention back to his work for the sake of other readers, those who are perhaps not yet familiar with him…

Bill's Confession

Let me begin right here. Why not?
I'm all fool and some,
Two in one, doctor and poet,
Yanking out babies, squalling,
On bright-shining mornings,
Closing the eyes of the dead
Clothed in their stinking rags
Behind closed curtains,
Those night calls are the most haunting…

But you know all that already,
What life amounts to,
The mud and the slime of this America,
That's what I'm going after,
And how any poet must tell his story

In a language new made for the purpose.
You couldn't reach me there.
You wouldn't dare.
Try living knuckle-bare
Amongst all those poor souls that I treated…

I'm no faker,
For all the japes and jocosity.
I picked that up from the poor,
Who never lie…
Nor do I neglect the small things in life,
Never could, never would, never should.

I want my poems to be made, always,
Of all the stuff hereabouts.
Trash – tin cans bowling, blown about rubbish –
Has its own ways of posing.
You hear me out on that one.
I'll write about what I damn well please.

The drink I'd give you,
Though I'm no great bibber,
If I were to choose it – here, take it –
Is the abiding sweetness of Sarsaparilla
Slipping down the throat.
There's nothing else like it.

Paterson, New Jersey,
That was my homeland,
Or call it my heartland maybe,
With all the filth of the Passaic River
Flowing through it in the 20s…

Orange, green, yellow water
So sluggish in its going,
Skimmed with the sheen of grease.
The kids used to swim in it…

Did I call it an 'unbridled leap'?
This writing thing, I mean.
That is what it all must amount to.
Poetry, in the end, is a thing unencumbered.
You wallow in river mud up to the ankles.

I'm going after this new measure.
Where to find it?
The variable foot,
That's what I once chose to call it,
A line just as long as it takes
A pair of ragged human lungs to breathe it.

I need to tell you
About the rough and tumble of the writing life,
How and when the words get written
On scraps of prescription paper
Or any old what-not,

How the sparks of a poem
Flare at midnight,
Of words and how they fall
And spill from the mouth,

In fits and starts
Often too fast to catch,
In spurts and hesitations…

I bang my feet
In time to the rhythms
When I hammer down on the keys…
The boys heard it. Flossie heard it.
Did she shut me up? She did not.

Breakfast – all except for Monday, when the place is closed – is taken on a high bar stool in Il Pozo des Frailes, the closest village to the house. The barman knows our habits. The coffees come fast and, my god, scalding hot…

At the Bar in Pozo

Mahou desde 1990
Are the words
Burnt into the wooden seats

Of the high bar stools
So neatly tucked into
The small table at which we're seated

Pert as birds on the look-out…
Bulbous wine glasses hang
In rows above the bar

Where the locals all sit
Slope-shouldered, huddled in chat
Letting us get on with it

Tostadas in the shape of
Boats long and lean
Arrive with omelets slopping off…

Over at the bar Pastis,
Squirted from the bottle
Clouds toughened glasses

One coffee's gone
We nod for the next
Two make for a perfect inner heat

Omelet grease
Oils the ends of fingers
I slip off the stool

Smile, and offer a note.
The bar man nods
Smiles are mutual. We're off.

Bill was a contested spirit. For years he found it difficult to get his poetry published except by small presses. He never really became part of the mainstream. He was finally awarded a Pulitzer Prize for a book of poems, but it was his very last book, and he was dead for the announcement.

The early collections were often little editions of fine quality, made by people prosperous enough to squander money on making beautiful books of poems. Money was never a part of the equation. It never would be for Bill either. He never became a writer full-time. He never gave up the doctoring. Fact is it was just as much a part of him as being a poet. What were his themes?Nature was one of them. He adored trees and flowers. He would take visitors to see his garden at the back of the house. His poems were often conversations with flowers, even tough-minded ones…

Cacti

Take these cacti, for example.
Do I love them?
No, I do not!

But they belong here – unlike me.
I fly in and then, days later, I leave,
In a swirl of kicked back, car-tyre dust…

Fact is I don't really like what I see…
Cacti are flat, splayed gloves
Of a leathery green

With pock-marked skin.
Snap one off, plant it, and it grows again.
Cacti die to live again

In this cruel, hard-bitten, arid land.
Their spines say: keep off!
I'm sufficient unto myself.

I'll never need you,
You, with your prissy watering cans.
Take off back where you came.

Cacti stare back, unflinching.
They could smack me about
Like a foul-mouthed boxer.

Connecticut Hemlocks

Show me again
Some Connecticut hemlocks.
I'll plant them

In front of the house
So I can look out on them
As if they were old friends.

They hum tunes at me
When I look at them,
Lull me when I'm half broken,

Gather up the pieces.
Hemlock, hemlock,
You came here when needed.

You always speak back
When spoken to
Not like some people

Bill liked to write about the broken, the imperfect, the unrefined, of how life, no matter how hard-bitten, had to be survived, perhaps even with a modicum of dignity. It was a matter of fighting through, fighting back against adversity. That's why he admired the poor, for their spirit, their lack of veneer or refinement, their straight talking. Life in the raw, life as a brawl, backs against the broken wall. The only thing left was to kick out. I'm thinking these thoughts on a warm spring evening in Andalucia, in a garden full of delicate lanterns prettifying a garden. The days are long here, even in springtime. The scene adds up to a beautiful illusion. Doesn't the stony landscape of Andalucia strive to humiliate all things human?

Bill often wrote about human relationships. The dialogues between man and wife in his plays could be bruising. His marriage to Flossie was long and good. They tolerated each other's imperfections. Bill had affairs. The marriage rumbled on. Flossie was tough-minded and sharp of tongue when need be. She kept all of Bill's published books in order, in a cabinet in his study. She knew what he'd done, and when he'd done it. She was a powerful gate-keeper, and he loved and admired her for it.

Going

1.

I left as soon as I needed.
You told me to go.
You were a bitch to do it.

I wanted a kid new made,
Sweet, clean and wholesome.
Our fresh plucked flower,

Our daylight wonder...
He'd belong to both of us.
Fat chance of that one.

Why so much trepidation?
You open your mouth
With another foul showing.

You owe me a lot, you know.
I caught you one time,
When you were falling!

You don't remember all that?
Are you stupid or something,
Leaning against that broken window?

2.

Nothing's changed about this place.
How could it, with you
Standing at the door, looking out

Hoping for...what exactly?
If you just once could tell me,
Things might get straightened out...

When I go out again,
You're leaning against the wall,
Blowing out smoke.

We barely see each other.
All the day's brightness
Is for someone else.

Marriage, what's it for in the end?
Small talk beside the stove.
A laugh or two in the bedroom.

Bill wanted to make a poetry that distilled the soul, the verbal mannerisms, the speech of America, that land of savagery, born in the violence of the conquistadores – he wrote a lot about the drag and the pain of that blood-soaked inheritance, so defining of the American character, in a book called *In the American Grain*, which was highly praised by D.H.Lawrence, a man Bill always wanted to meet because he thought they had a lot in common. They never did.

Coincidences can be so hauntingly strange. I was reading that book one sunny morning in April, having just returned to London from the house in Andalucia. My eye fell upon these sentences, a snatching of words from the journal of an ever restless, never sufficiently satisfied, sea-voyaging conquistador: 'From this day and ever afterward, very temperate breezes, so that there was great pleasure in enjoying the mornings, nothing being wanted but the song of the nightingale. It was like April in Andalucia.' Bill was quoting those words from the journal of Christopher Columbus, written at the end of the fifteenth century.

He never stopped brooding on the singularity of the lives of the poor and the disadvantaged, in his prose and his poetry. Those voyagers on *The Mayflower*, he wrote, possessed 'the collective sense of the destiny common to lowly people'. And also to reflect on the bloody birth of the nation of which he was a part: 'To impersonate…the very primitive itself' can be a source of a 'terrific ungoverned strength…' Out of such needling doubts and fears he fashioned many fine poems.

My Cussed Land

There has to be
This United States way of writing.
That's what I'm after

To set it all down
Straight from the mouth
Cussings and all

Breathing it, spitting it out
Hearing you speak
As you do from the side of the mouth

The drag and the drawl
The sneer and the whine
As they fall at your feet

Words rough as stones
Piled in a heap
Beside a road brawling with traffic

The blare of all that night noise
Up the avenues of Manhattan
When you kind of forget to sleep

Extracurricular

'My own interest in the arts has been extracurricular. Up from the gutter, so to speak.' From introduction to the *Collected Later Poems*

Come and go as you please.
Make light of it.
Life, that is.

We took it all!
At least, that's what you said,
Being brazen and a hothead.

I was never so sure.
I hung about on the corner,
Collar bladed against fine rain.

Maybe we're both monkeys in a cage,
Stuffing in the food
Until it stops, and then we rage.

Did you ever cry in your sleep?
As a child, you say,
Shamelessly...

Peggy

Peggy the cat is beating the bounds
Of the garden, delicate stepping,
Aloof and prideful

As any pretty girl trying to be noticed.
She haunts the kitchen when hungry –
One leap and she's a shawl around the shoulders.

Ouch! Painful as hell!
Come on now, Peggy, you say,
In a whisper of exasperation,

Lifting her off,
Before filling up the bowl
With stinking cat meat.

She's a beauty though.
When the TV screen glows of an evening,
She poses, long legs so neat, for hours on end, pure Ancient Egypt.

Lawrence

He had that smell
Of a beast about him
And I loved him for it.

He saw danger in all things,
The roughness of life's edges,
Restless, lunging.

I wish I'd met him
But he was too far south
For me to travel

So I pin his picture up here
On this cork-board in the study.
I watch his leanness,

And the way he bows his head
When walking forward,
Not wanting to be noticed.

To me he had that look
Of a bolting ferret about him.
No, I never saw his teeth.

Bill delivered many babies, and his most famous novel, *White Mule,* begins with the birth of a baby. The scene raises up the event until it almost becomes a scene from Botticelli. The truth was often much more abject, sad, and blighted by poverty or the heartless or careless behaviour of menfolk. Bill did his best with the meagre means at his disposal.

Whadya call her that for?

Whadya call her that for?
Let me hold her, babes.
Don't keep me from her.

It makes me laugh
That face all squished up
Like balled paper.

I never said that
To hurt you.
I just couldn't help it.

Isn't this a joyous moment?
Why the curtains closed?
Do you really want that?

There's sun out there.
Your mother's comin over.
Let's split this beer for god's sake.

There is always rivalry in any community of poets. They earn so little. What do they have to lose but their meagre and hotly contested (by each other, that is) reputations? Even the most famous have to take teaching jobs to put food on the table. Bill's profession, on the other hand, was solid, and that's how he wanted it to be. The writing was always done on borrowed time. What is more, the profession of doctor and obstetrician gave him material for his writing, precious insights into human vagaries and human tragedies. As an outsider – he always regarded himself in that way, even when he became feted as a poet in old age – Bill nurtured his envies and his jealousies like the rest of us. He was very much aware of the reputations of celebrated insiders such as Wallace Stevens and T.S. Eliot. Nothing could have delighted him more than the decision by Wallace Stevens to use one of his short poems – he gobbled it up whole – as the epigraph to a poem in *Harmonium*, Stevens's first book, the poem that begins: 'It's a strange courage you give me, ancient star…' One remark by Stevens made Bill bristle. He called Bill's poetry 'anti-poetic'. By contrast with the suaveness, the studied literary elegance and the lofty intellectual teasing of Stevens, you could say that there is some truth to that charge. Bill's poems seem rough, spiky and worldly by contrast.

The case of T.S.Eliot was of quite a different nature, and the animosity much more profound and longer lasting. Bill never forgave Eliot for decamping to London, assuming the identity of a cultivated European, and then, the worst offence of all, for writing *The Waste Land*. Well, it was not so much the writing of it as the wide and almost immediate recognition that it received as a masterpiece of Modernism. Was it not Bill himself, he who had stayed at home in New Jersey, who was the exemplar of the modern manner, who was trying to make a new kind of poetry fit for the current moment? What is more, the appearance of *The Waste Land* in 1921 seemed to Bill like a double betrayal. Bill's old friend Ezra Pound had also decamped to Europe and, what is more, it was he who had taken in hand, quite brilliantly, the editing of the *The Waste Land*, with Eliot's acquiescence, cutting out, quite ruthlessly, so much that was superfluous, and in fact turning it into the masterpiece that it finally became. Bill and Eliot never met. Bill detested the man life-long because he had been eclipsed by a man he regarded as a smoothly operating traitor. He also carried on surveying the world that he knew.

Night Scene

Long long the light stays on
In this room in Rutherford
Where I make these songs of mine

Small things, but needful,
Tough-minded
As roots tenacious…

I go to it when I can
Too little time for the writing game,
Life, life always pushing back again…

Kids brawl in their filthy rags
A man showing up with a gangrenous leg
Do something about that, Doc, he says –

For a bundle of vegetables
From the garden plot…
What else did he have? I'm asking you

When the Twister Came

When the twister came
Everything got thrown about like crazy
It was hell's mouth and more in New Jersey

Bodies fences trucks got bowled over
Rolling down the road
Light as a feather

I just ran from house to house
Dodging fallen branches
Doing what I could, never enough

The old woman with a leg trapped
Squeezed up between wall and truck
I thrust a chloroform-soaked wad

Into her face to put her out
As the truck got lifted off her leg
And we dragged her off

Laid her down in her own garden plot
Flinging her arms about, moaning
Until she stopped breathed her last breath out…

God above rest her
On that day
To forever remember

Escapology

Escapology

Not be rightly spoken of.

Not to accommodate any element of trust,
which slips through the fingers
at every moment of chance encounter.

Not to say to you, yes,
and to another, surely not.

Not to be alive in this moment,
but to have flittered away
on the wing without rancour.

Not to own a house in the suburbs,
but to carry a sack on a back,
as if a delivery man without care or pretensions.

Not to berate the multitudes with false certitudes,
but to whistle a tune or two,
Extemporising willy nilly *as the wind listeth*.

Not to be accountable for the truth-telling of liars,
or the unbounded admiration accorded
to church deacons and certain football managers.

Not to go anywhere too soon,
but to stay put here,
So that when stumbled over,

the man or the woman looks a little startled,
as if to ask: what held you then?
Could it have been nothing other than

the pull of the moon behind distant cloud-cover?

Pigeons Hugger-Muggering

To make these idle and refractory words
stand to attention this morning
is almost more than I am capable of,

so I may as well lie back down on this sofa
and count the dust motes as they fall
into my be-startled eye…

What else is there to be done
on such a morning as this one,
with the air so still across the whole of London

and these two fat pigeons on the garden fence
up and about at their usual nonsense?

Puffed Out
for my valentine

God alone knows what must have happened to us both.
We'd waited long enough for it all to take shape.
You changed your clothes, repeatedly,
because you could never quite get it just so

as I sat, a little helpless, on the bed side,
not knowing how best to interpose myself.
When you stepped out later it was, as ever,
unrepeatable, and no one else would have known…

I think of those things now, that silk top, or
those Berlin trousers at whose price tag I baulked,
puffed out in such an unexpectedly stylish way,
with me standing beside you, a scarecrow off of a Sheffield lane.

Beside the Road in the Catskills

The mist had cleared by noon.
Tables were lifted out into the sunshine.
Those who had been standing around in hope
sat down with sighs of pleasure.
The traffic movement had been constant.

The mountain peaks were visible again –
by which I mean the moulded tree line
because there were always
trees in such abundance.

We, being people of the valley,
looked up in that general direction,
no more than that,
forever sun-blessed and motionless
(or so it seemed just then).

Uniquely Disaffected

The last gift to go was by far the most precious.
I handed it over with great reluctance
to a man whose sorrow knew no bounds,
a man whose presence had only then
                made itself known to me.

Why then give a gift to a man unknown?
Why reserve that most precious moment of bestowal
for he whose life you had never known, let alone understood
                or sympathised with?

Did he accept it with pleasure?
Did he step forward when it became evident
                that it would be proffered?
Did you see bewilderment or dismay in his eyes
as his hands rose up, stiff as clockwork, to grasp it?
Did he stall just then, uniquely disaffected?

Gaffer
for Cynthia

Gaffer, being a man of the people,
Walked in front of her, always.
He knew how to lead,
being a blazing idealist
of a thoroughly left-wing persuasion.
Annie Besant was grandma's consolation.

It was his own green bench that
we brought down here from Manchester,
in the van, to sit on,
in our garden here in Kent.
John and I used to say to each other:
I cannot imagine anything better than this,
with Gaffer saying the words after.

The last time I saw him,
he came shuffling past his own dinner table
where all of us were gathered.
'Behold thy father's ghost,' he muttered, in passing.
Disraeli and Gladstone always rang in his ears.
You see, he was an orator manqué.
The first time I met him
he gave me this precious copy
of Shaw's *Man and Superman*.
It's yours if you will have it.

The Licence

Your licence is to kill me.
I give it now,
Crisply, with hand shake,
Not wishing to put off
That moment when
Satisfaction will overcome you.

And now the deed is done.
You and yours look on,
Relieved that my voice
No longer commands the air,
Laughing at all that you are,
Calling you a fool twice over.

May you sleep sound,
My sometime friend,
Until the sleep of death
Overcomes you,
When we shall meet again,
And revenge be sweet
Because least expected.

Sailing with the Voyagers

I have sailed with the voyagers
In times past, and I shall do so again.
Wave to me at the pier's side as I leave.
Do not trouble if I do not turn back
And give you in return a final wave
Of farewell. You know my going mood.

You know it is my purpose
Always to be leaving. A leave-taking man
When he returns, forever looks back
To the waters on which his boat has churned,
Seeing her again breasting the waves,
Feeling his stomach heave
With the upcoming bounce of the waves.

And when he returns, there is impatience
In his tread, always, the way his boots pound
The hard and fast pavements, loud and unceasing,
Vexed and forever impatient.
Expect nothing better of me then.
Let me sail with the voyagers without pity.

Sin

An inability to see as far as
        the door, or,
Once having found the door, a
        refusal
To open it – or perhaps an
        inability to recognise
Of what wood it is made.

And then, having grappled with
        he door,
An inability to throw it down, or
        to say:
There, door, are you on the
        ground, and,
Here, door, am I, standing above
        you.

In fact, to say instead: a door is a
        makeshift thing,
A thing of wood, a nothing of a
        presence.
And yet, for all that, to be refused,
        by the presence
Of the door, entrance to further
        things.

And to know the howling
        frustrations
Of being denied admission by
        such as
This door, of the kind that you see
        too,
And bear away on your back, bent
        double.

Thirst

Thirst

It was a thirsting after knowing
what your face would amount to
were I to paint it after all
without your knowing…

Did you sit in the window,
listening out for a something
that would define you again,
something fresh, sharply figured?

My eyes probed, again and again.
I wanted you to know me.
I wanted to ask you the questions
you would readily answer.

You sat perfectly still,
contained in your silence
which wrapped you about,
and I dared not enter.

I stood at the doorway,
the soul of hesitation,
carrying it all, like a something,
too readily shattered…

In profile I see you,
lips somewhat parted,
eyes forfending the light,
eye-lids lit, bulbous…